THE BAFFLED PARENT'S G

COACHING GI

LACROSSE

Look for these other Baffled Parent's Guides from Ragged Mountain Press

Coaching Youth Baseball: The Baffled Parent's Guide,
by Bill Thurston

Great Baseball Drills: The Baffled Parent's Guide,
by Jim Garland

Coaching Youth Basketball: The Baffled Parent's Guide,
by David G. Faucher

Great Basketball Drills: The Baffled Parent's Guide,
by Jim Garland

Coaching Youth Football: The Baffled Parent's Guide,
by Paul Pasqualoni with Jim McLaughlin

Teaching Kids Golf: The Baffled Parent's Guide,
by Detty Moore

Coaching Boys' Lacrosse: The Baffled Parent's Guide,
by Greg Murrell and Jim Garland

Coaching Youth Soccer: The Baffled Parent's Guide,
by Bobby Clark

Great Soccer Drills: The Baffled Parent's Guide,
by Tom Fleck and Ron Quinn

Coaching Youth Softball: The Baffled Parent's Guide,
by Jacquie Joseph

Coaching Tee Ball: The Baffled Parent's Guide,
by Bing Broido

THE BAFFLED PARENT'S

GUIDE TO

COACHING GIRLS'

LACROSSE

Janine Tucker

with Maryalice Yakutchik

Ragged Mountain Press/McGraw-Hill

Camden, Maine • New York • Chicago • San Francisco
Lisbon • London • Madrid • Mexico City • Milan • New Delhi
San Juan • Seoul • Singapore • Sydney • Toronto

To my husband John—the most amazing coach I have ever met, and my inspiration. To my sons Ryan and Devin—may your involvement in sports bring you as much joy as you have brought me. To my mom and dad—who encouraged me at every turn. To Diane—you are my hero.

JANINE TUCKER

To those who have coached me in writing and lacrosse, especially Joan Mellen and Tina Sloan Green. And, of course, to those who coach me every day in life: Brian, Caroline, and Brian Wensel. Also, in memory of my mother, Regina Yakutchik, who sat shivering and cheering through countless lacrosse games.

MARYALICE YAKUTCHIK

The McGraw·Hill Companies

7 8 9 0 DOC DOC 0 9 8

Copyright © 2003 by Ragged Mountain Press

Library of Congress Cataloging-in-Publication Data
Tucker, Janine.
  The baffled parent's guide to coaching girls' lacrosse / Janine Tucker with Maryalice Yakutchik.
        p.   cm.—(The baffled parent's guides)
Includes bibliographical references (p.   ) and index.
  ISBN 0-07-141225-5
  1. Lacrosse for girls—Coaching. 2. Lacrosse for girls—Training. I. Yakutchik, Maryalice. II. Title. III. Series.
  GV989.15.T83 2003
  796.347′082—dc21   2002154251

Questions regarding the content of this book should be addressed to
Ragged Mountain Press
P.O. Box 220
Camden, ME 04843
www.raggedmountainpress.com

Questions regarding the ordering of this book should be addressed to
The McGraw-Hill Companies
Customer Service Department
P.O. Box 547
Blacklick, OH 43004
Retail customers: 1-800-262-4729
Bookstores: 1-800-722-4726

Photographs by David Sanders unless otherwise noted.
Illustrations by George Arentz.

Contents

Introduction

So, you're a Baffled Parent.

You thought you were going to drop off your daughter at the recreation center for a meeting about the upcoming lacrosse season, maybe hang around in the background until the teams were picked. Before you knew what was happening, you found yourself "appointed" coach of one of the teams, though "captured" might be a more appropriate verb. Your weak protest—"I've never even seen a women's lacrosse game, much less played in one"—fell on deaf ears. Your admission that you've never, ever coached anything in your life earned you sympathetic smiles and wishes of good luck from all around.

Now you're in for it!

Don't despair. Help is at hand. In fact, help is in your hands. This book is designed to help all coaches—neophytes as well as those with years of experience. Maryalice played high school, college, and club lacrosse and has coached at the youth level for several years, so she thought she knew something about coaching lacrosse. Ha! A mere half-hour into the first meeting with Janine to brainstorm the contents of this book, she was full of energy and new ideas and literally champing at the bit to begin coaching her sixth season of youth lacrosse—hopefully the most successful to date. And by "successful," we don't just mean more wins than losses. The advice and drills here are aimed at helping you teach girls the basics of lacrosse, sportsmanship, and teamwork while having fun in "the fastest game on two feet."

In addition to being inherently safe and wildly fun, lacrosse holds the distinction of being the oldest sport in America. It dates back centuries. Native Americans used playing sticks and a ball to resolve conflicts and heal the sick. "Fields" ranged from 1 to 15 miles in length, and "games" would last for days. Where the game had its origin is anybody's guess; it could have been transported to the North American coast via the Norsemen who played a similar sport in Iceland in the ninth century.

Women's lacrosse was born in Britain in the late 1800s. An early pioneer of women's lacrosse internationally, Scottish-born Rosabelle Sinclair was dubbed the American Grand Dame of Lacrosse. In his book *Lacrosse: A History of the Game*, Donald M. Fisher quotes Sinclair as saying: "Lacrosse, as girls play it, is an orderly pastime that has little in common with the men's tribal-warfare version except the long-handled racket or crosse that gives the sport its name. It's true that the object in both men's and women's lacrosse is to send a ball through a goal by means of the racket, but whereas the men resort to brute strength the women depend solely on skill."

Who is playing the game today and what game are they playing? There are more than 125,000 youth players nationwide, according to US Lacrosse, the national governing body of men's and women's lacrosse. That's not counting 100,000+ high school players, 20,000+ college players, and thousands of postcollegiate club players.

An extraordinary number of these lacrosse players are women. A true

Lacrosse is the fastest game on two feet.

life sport, women's lacrosse can take a girl nearly from the cradle to the rocking chair. And it could earn her a college education along the way: There are more collegiate women's lacrosse programs than men's, and the women's version of the sport is growing at a more rapid pace than the men's game. Men's and women's lacrosse are two distinct forms of the same game, played under different rules. Women's rules limit stick contact, prohibit body contact, and, therefore, require little protective equipment. Lacrosse sometimes is perceived to be a violent game, but injury statistics prove otherwise. In fact, it's among the safest athletic activities when compared to other sports such as soccer and basketball. Speaking of those popular games, lacrosse combines many elements of soccer and basketball. The fast-paced play attracts and appeals to athletes, coaches, and spectators. The game requires and rewards coordination and agility; quickness and speed are key.

The fastest growing segment of the lacrosse world is at the youth level. The number of youth players, ages 12 and under, is exploding. That's why we're writing this book. There's an incredible demand for more teams, more leagues, more coaches. "The game has grown so much that we haven't been able to keep up with it in terms of quality coaches and umpires," says Pat Dillon, Rules Chair of the Women's Division of US Lacrosse. With this in mind, we developed *Coaching Girls' Lacrosse: The Baffled Parent's Guide*. Our mission is to help beginning and experienced coaches successfully teach the game of women's lacrosse—using the most progressive tactics in the game today.

How to Use This Book

This hands-on guide, with its contemporary approach to the fast-moving and ever-changing game of lacrosse, is dedicated to developing and inspiring girls' lacrosse coaches at the youth level, novice through advanced.

The main purpose is first to put a stick into the hands of all those who love to see girls enjoying the game of lacrosse, and then to give them the tools necessary for passionately teaching the most progressive skills and techniques in the game today. This book recognizes and celebrates that today's girls' game is vastly different from the game of just five years ago, from the design and handling of the sticks to the field setup right down to the very heart of the game: the offensive and defensive strategies. The best part, and yet the most challenging aspect, of coaching girls' lacrosse is that the game continues to evolve as the athleticism, speed, and skill of the players improve. This requires coaches to stay a step ahead. This book is the key to doing just that. Women's lacrosse is exploding nationally and internationally, and this book establishes a consistent and proven method for coaches everywhere to teach a game that is played not only at the youth level but also at the high school and collegiate levels and beyond. The style of play and the skills that this book teaches will last girls throughout their entire lacrosse careers, whether they simply want to enjoy a couple years of recreational play or progress to the point of traveling with the U.S. Women's Lacrosse team to defend the cup in world championship play.

Chapter 1, Then and Now, outlines and embraces recent—and dramatic—changes in the sport. Women's lacrosse today is very different than it was just a few years ago. The next several chapters will help the novice coach get started. Chapter 2, Creating an Atmosphere of Good Habits, gives coaches concrete examples to help them organize and control team behavior while creating a positive atmosphere through high energy and enthusiastic reinforcement. Chapter 3, Before Hitting the Field: Girls' Lacrosse in a Nutshell, deals with the specific rules and regulations of each of the various age levels of girls' youth lacrosse, as well as equipment and field specifications for each age level: 6 to 8 (Under 9); 9 to 10 (Under 11); and 11 to 12 (Under 13). Chapter 4, Setting Up the Season, deals with the best way to involve the parents, choose an assistant, draw up a checklist for the season, and get necessary coaching equipment. Chapter 5, Essential Skills: A Progressive Approach, teaches the basic skills of girls' lacrosse—such as cradling—in a progressive style using a confidence-building approach. Chapter 6, The Fundamentals of Offense, covers the concepts necessary to develop a successful team offense, while chapter 7, The Fundamentals of Defense, develops team defensive concepts. Chapter 8, The Practice, sets forth the components of a successful practice, in a general sense. It also includes a sample four-week practice outline. Chapter 9, Game Day, reviews what to expect during a game and provides an overview of game format as well as how to handle substitutions, time-outs, and injuries. Chapter 10, FUN-damental Drills Are Fun!, gives coaches creative and active drills for developing fundamental skills while keeping practices lively and fun. General skills include throwing, catching, scooping, dodging, shooting, and stick-work tricks. Chapters 11 and 12 provide concepts and drills that replicate game situations for the offense and defense. The all-important chapter 13 addresses a long-neglected position at the youth level, the goalie.

Included are umpire signals, a glossary of "lax talk," where you'll find definitions of many of the terms we use in this book, a list of resources available to you, and a detailed index.

Developing a Coaching Style

We don't want parents to be intimidated or have reservations about getting involved as coaches in youth programs. Coaching is teaching, plain and simple. Parents are natural teachers of their own kids. Dubious though you may be, you too have teaching skills that can be transferred into a coaching environment. Trust your instincts. Successful coaches are good teachers who infuse lessons with positive motivation. Effective teachers have the ability to break down their subject matter into easy-to-understand components. This book is all about breaking down the game of lacrosse into components that you can teach and then build on. We assure you that a great coaching style will emerge if you

- come to practice prepared
- maintain a positive approach
- stay flexible
- show enthusiasm
- get to know your players as individuals and as a team

Broadly speaking, beginner drills and games are developmentally appropriate for ages 6 to 8; intermediate, for ages 9 and 10; and advanced, for ages 11 and 12.

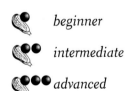

beginner

intermediate

advanced

We've used these symbols to help guide you in the selection of drills in chapters 10 to 13. However, you must keep in mind that kids learn the game and develop their motor skills at different ages. Use the drills and games that best fit the needs of your team and your individual players, regardless of their age. We encourage you to encourage your players to challenge themselves at every practice. Teach them what the "big girls" learn and don't hold back because they're young . . . they can do it!

No book hoping to offer coaching advice will work unless it recognizes the differences, sometimes quite obvious, in your players' abilities and responses to coaching. There is no one right way to coach, but there are wrong approaches.

We, as coaches and authors, align ourselves with the Positive Coaching Alliance, the mission of which is "transforming youth sports so sports can transform youth." We join the PCA in our desire to spark and fuel a "social epidemic" of Positive Coaching that will sweep lacrosse fields around the country. The vision of the PCA is to create a sports culture in which kids love to play the game, look forward to practices and games, and retain that joy throughout their lives. Universally, people react positively to encouragement and praise. But simply being encouraging isn't quite enough. We'll show you how to handle all kinds of situations that you'll encounter while coaching girls' lacrosse.

Who We Are

Janine Tucker is the head women's lacrosse coach at Johns Hopkins University, a position she's held for ten years. Under her leadership, the team was elevated in 1998 from Division III to Division I and became a nationally ranked top 20 team. In her first year at Johns Hopkins, the team record was 16–1, the best record in the school's history. Her overall record is 111–40. At the Division III Level, she was an Intercollegiate Women's Lacrosse Coaches Association (IWLCA) South Region Coach of the Year for four years. She has coached thirteen All-Americans, along with four Division III Centennial Conference Players of the Year. In addition, Janine has developed and directed girls' lacrosse camps for over a decade, instructing players at every level from 6-year-old beginners to collegiate All-Americans. She also enjoys speaking at clinics nationwide for youth, high school, and collegiate coaches. Prior to Johns Hopkins, she was the assistant women's lacrosse coach at Loyola College, where she was an All-American lacrosse player in 1989. She is a member of the Loyola College Athletic Hall of Fame and was recently inducted into the US Lacrosse Hall of Fame, Greater Baltimore chapter. She graduated in 1989 from Loyola College with a bachelor's degree in communications.

Maryalice Yakutchik is a freelance journalist who writes regularly for the Discovery Channel. Her live expeditions about wildlife and culture appear regularly on Discovery.com and AnimalPlanet.com. She also writes for traditional print media, including newspapers and magazines such as the *Philadelphia Inquirer, Los Angeles Times, Boston Globe, USA Today, Islands,* and *Defenders of Wildlife*. She currently teaches journalism courses at Loyola College. As a student at Temple University (Division I, NCAA) Maryalice was awarded a four-year athletic scholarship for varsity lacrosse and earned a bachelor's degree in journalism and a master's degree in creative writing. She has coached women's lacrosse on the college level, but for the past six years she has devoted her spring seasons to coaching recreation league lacrosse for 6- to 12-year-old girls in her hometown of Monkton, Maryland.

CHAPTER 1

Then and Now

At Janine Tucker's girls' summer lacrosse camp, 6-year-old Gabrielle had tears of joy in her eyes when, after 20 minutes of desperately trying to toss the ball behind her back and catch it between her legs—like the big girls do—she mastered this very cool stick trick. The smile never left her face as she continued to do it for the rest of the night. (See pages 109–15 for more stick tricks.)

They Can Do It!

Don't sell your players short just because they happen to be short—and young and female. You'll be surprised at how quickly youth players can pick up and master advanced techniques. If you treat them like athletes, you'll find yourself thinking of them as athletes, and they'll find themselves performing like athletes. The fact that they happen to be young girls will become a mere afterthought to you and, more importantly, to them.

We're convinced that the men's game is at the level it is because of consistent teaching up through the ranks. Janine could take any seven lacrosse-playing boys and put them on a field with a ball and say, "Set up a four-on-three fast break," and the defenders immediately would know how to position themselves, and so would the attackers. Everyone would be in sync, and their performance would mimic that of college players because boys learn men's lacrosse.

Not so with girls. The challenge as we see it is to teach young girls a universal game called "women's lacrosse." Far too often girls still learn "girls' lacrosse" instead of a universal game that will see them through their entire careers. We're talking style, not rules. Certainly, different rules apply to different levels of play as well as age brackets. Obviously, you need to play within the rules. But what rule says that a 6-year-old can't shoot behind her back? None. What rule says a cradle has to travel awkwardly across the body? None. We believe girls should be taught early on the correct way to execute ad-

Everybody wins when
everybody plays.

vanced skills—such as checking—even though youth rules prevent them
from checking in games. The foundation for the proper execution of skills
needs to be laid early on, when the girls are eager to do what is asked of them.

    Girls' lacrosse has been taught in a "traditional" style for a long time—
too long. We are encouraging coaches now to get "unstuck" from tradition
for tradition's sake, to embrace the more progressive style of play that has
emerged over the past half-dozen years, and to start teaching this style to
the youngest players instead of waiting until some ambiguous age when
"they're ready."

    Clearly, the reason most people still cling to and teach the old style is
that they haven't yet been taught or developed an appreciation for the progressive style of women's lacrosse. The progressive style is flashier, tougher,
more physical, and more aggressive. Some would argue more dangerous.
(But it's not.) It requires of players a mastery of sophisticated skills in stick
handling as well as the ability to be creative—to think outside the box. It
challenges players to try the wildest stick trick or shot just for the sake of
"I can do this, and it's fun!"

Within the last six years, the game of women's lacrosse has drastically changed. Everything—from the look and setup of the field to the handling of the stick to the very stick itself—has evolved. A lot of the changes have to do with girls coming into their own as hardcore athletes. Women's lacrosse has been influenced by the men's game in subtle and not so subtle ways; they aren't all negative. The commitment to developing opportunity for women in sport, the catalyst of which was Title IX, has changed the game irrevocably.

Why teach a 7-year-old youth player a more traditional and conservative style of lacrosse, one that won't challenge her as much as a more progressive style and one that won't see her through her entire career if she chooses to stick with lacrosse? Our challenge to you, as a youth coach, is to start each girl's development down the progressive path the moment she picks up a stick and begins to cradle.

For far too long we thwarted our own progress and stinted our growth as lacrosse players by teaching youth players differently than we would teach high school girls. We'd teach them the big, wide awkward cradle when they're young, only to reinstruct them later to relax the cradle. There are skills and drills in this book that are challenging, and maybe even controversial when taught to younger players. But we feel the need to start young girls developing, learning, and polishing the same techniques they'll use at the highest level of the game.

As mentioned, 6- to 12-year-old female athletes are eager to learn. They will do what is asked and will eagerly emulate what you show them. Why teach a stiff, rigid style of the game to them as recreational players, only to expect them to dramatically shift that style of play in high school? Instead of wasting time knocking down what they've learned and having to rebuild, they'll simply keep building and building throughout their careers.

Consistency is the key. As if you couldn't tell, we're proponents of a universal style of lacrosse. In this book, we're proposing that you teach your daughters and their friends a universal way to play that will be appropriate whether they're on youth teams or the World Cup team: same techniques, same skills, same tactics. A big, huge, rigid cradle wastes an 8-year-old's energy and impedes her ability to move the ball quickly just as much as it does an 18-year-old's. Try teaching them from the get-go a smooth, soft-handed cradle that is multilevel, relaxed, and precise. It's bound to grow on them—as well as with them.

Here are some quick hits comparing and contrasting women's lacrosse then and now.

Then: Every March, girls took sticks and kilts out of mothballs. They practiced a couple of times a week and played an eight-game season, after which they put away the sticks until next spring. That was it.

Now: Players are handling their sticks year-round in organized and unorganized play. Sticks aren't just for playing lacrosse games; they're for having fun, for performing tricks that develop hand-eye coordination. Girls are encouraged to achieve a heightened comfort with their sticks by handling the ball at many levels, for instance, and switching hands without thinking about it. Their sticks become extensions of their arms.

Then: Safety was the main concern.

Now: Safety is still the main concern.

Then: Lacrosse was an exclusive upper-crust sport confined to wide-open rolling green fields and thus was the dynasty of that limited segment of the population who had access to such fields. The style of play was genteel and mannerly. Proper, even.

Now: The players are bigger, stronger, faster, more dedicated. And every year there are more of them than ever, playing in every nook and cranny not only in this country but also abroad. Women play lacrosse on postage-stamp fields in the inner cities of America. They play in Japan. The level of intensity is high: all players, across the board, are rewarded for aggressiveness as well as finesse.

Then: Ho-hum shooting. There was an overhand shot, a shovel shot, and not a whole lot else. The limited style of sticks—wooden—limited players' abilities to be creative when cradling or shooting the ball.

Now: *How'd she do that?!* Creativity is key. Anything goes when it comes to shooting at the goal. Goalies need to be prepared for shots coming from all angles on the field at every conceivable speed and from any distance. The differences in shooting then and now can be attributed to the development of a limitless (and often dizzying) variety of sticks—offset stick heads and deeper pockets allow for high-velocity shots and multilevel ball handling—and the players' ability to handle these sticks has improved tremendously.

Then: What stick tricks? There's no such thing . . .

Now: Players are encouraged to toss and pop and twirl and dip and weave the stick and the ball to develop hand-eye coordination. Unorthodox passes and catches give girls a whole new way to handle their stick with comfort, ease, and joy.

Then: The stick was wooden and handmade. The pocket was woven catgut with leather thongs. It took a long time to break in, and the fact that each stick was unique (and imperfectly balanced) made it challenging to replace if it became lost or cracked.

Now: Wooden sticks are still available, but mass-manufactured plastic-headed sticks with handles of aluminum or titanium are hands down the most popular styles on lacrosse fields today. Among the cutting-edge sticks are those with very thin sidewalls, which allow for much deeper pockets, which, in turn, increase ball-handling ability and the velocity of shots.

Then: Lacrosse has never been an equipment-dependent sport. That's one of the things that makes it attractive to schools, recreation programs, and parents. All a girl ever needed was a stick, a ball, and a mouth guard.

Now: Lacrosse still is not an equipment-dependent sport. However, as the athletes become bigger, stronger, faster, and more aggressive, and as stick technology continues to influence the game, there is heated debate about mandating protective equipment, specifically eyewear (see sidebar, opposite).

Then: The cradle—which simulated the opening and closing of a gate—was a big, exaggerated motion across the body, requiring awkward wrist and arm position; it wasted time and energy. Players were instructed to grip the stick just below the head—using a tight top hand—by making a V with their thumb and index finger; then to twist the stick on the strong side of their body with the upper arm swanlike, elbow jutting out; and finally to execute a full cradle, which meant pulling the stick all the way across the body (a contorted position from which very few could pass or shoot) and then bringing it all the way back. The arms were stiff and rigid. It was not easily mastered.

Then and now: Wood sticks and plastic sticks still meet on today's lacrosse fields.

Left: The old-style cradle uses a V-grip of the top hand and a swanlike elbow jutting out.

Maryalice Yakutchik

Right: An awkward pull across the body characterizes the old-style cradle.

Maryalice Yakutchik

Protective Equipment

"The issue is the potential for catastrophic injury," says Pat Dillon, Rules Chair for US Lacrosse. "Eye protection is an option and is being tested on the college level as we look for a quality product. So, as soon as it's practicable . . . It's already mandated in New York and in Massachusetts by their state high school sports associations and the National Federation for High School Sports."

"I think helmets would encourage rougher play: intentional hitting and body contact," says Tina Sloan Green, author of *Modern Women's Lacrosse*. "It's up to the officials to decide how much incidental body contact is going to be allowed. Loose officiating means more contact. I think we need to pay more attention to officiating. I wouldn't want to see more intentional contact, but going after a ball and being aggressive while going after the draw, there's bound to be some contact. Aggressive is different than rough."

The sport of women's lacrosse without protective equipment is inherently safe, according to NCAA injury data. This is especially true at the youth level, where the modified checking rule keeps sticks away from the head. However, protective eyewear will most likely be universally mandated in the near future.

Now: The cradle is a lean, subtle motion that extends from ear to nose; it needs a relaxed arm and wrist and conserves energy. Players are instructed to use a soft and smooth rocking motion on one side of their body, so they are ready to pass or shoot in an instant.

The progressive cradle is loose and relaxed and relies more on wrist motion than on the arm.

Maryalice on Getting Physical

I took my Lightning girls' lacrosse team (ages 9 and 10) on a midseason field trip to a Division I women's lacrosse game between Johns Hopkins and Ohio Universities. I smiled as I heard the girls talking among themselves, first about how they liked Coach Tucker's fashionable high heels (which didn't hamper her a bit as she trotted up and down a rainslicked sideline) and second, about how strong, tough, and aggressive Tucker's college players were. As a former Division I lacrosse player for Temple University—a team that was notoriously aggressive—I, too, was in awe of the sheer athleticism of Tucker's team. I watched in amazement at the physicality of the game. I realized, as did my girls, that this is what our youth players face as they develop in the sport. Physical, aggressive play defines the contemporary game, as do the time-honored attributes of finesse and skill.

Like it or not, that's the way it is.

A couple of years back, I was coaching Tykers (ages 6 to 8). My co-coach was an intense but well-meaning dad who had played the sport in college and still played on the club level. His daughter was a meek, retiring sort who, with my own daughter, preferred plucking buttercups on the field to chasing down ground balls. After informing the girls that he was going to "be mad at them" if they didn't come up with the ground ball, he told them to use their elbows and hips to gain an advantage over their opponents. They stared at him wide-eyed and fearful.

I glared at him, biting my tongue. However, I realized while watching the Hopkins–Ohio game that my girls might indeed benefit from learning they could mix it up a little, as long as nothing they did was intentionally hurtful or mean. It's not bad for our young girls to learn they can be tough in the face of incidental contact.

We are *not* pointing an accusatory finger at the dads (and moms!) out there who are encouraging their young lacrosse players to use their bodies to protect the ball or to dip their shoulders in when going full tilt for a ground ball. These tactics characterize aggressive play. There's nothing wrong with that, as long as we're not crossing the line—meaning intentional and illegal use of the body or stick. The heart of the matter is the ability to execute skills *under control.* We have no problem with encouraging the aggressive execution of skills like cutting off defenders to pick up ground balls, firing off shots as hard as they can, or attempting good, hard checks, as long as the skills are executed under control.

Who's responsible for control? First and foremost, each girl is responsible for self-control, says Pat Dillon. A player must be accountable for her own actions. Who holds her accountable? Youth coaches have to keep up-to-date on the rules (which are reevaluated every year by a special subcommittee of US Lacrosse) and, in any given season, stay consistent about what they're teaching and how they're teaching it.

The officials, of course, are the ultimate point of control. Officials need to take charge, have a commanding presence on the field, and give good direction to players as they are being called for fouls. Officials are teachers, too, especially youth officials. They must respect aggressive play while maintaining control and staying consistent as the girls learn the right way to play the game safely, if aggressively.

Aggressive play can be fun and safe; incidental body-to-body contact might inadvertently happen when teams are playing hard—although there's never an excuse for intentional body-to-body or stick-to-body contact.

We believe wholeheartedly that it's good to help a girl learn early on that she can be tough. But let's acknowledge that there's another side. Contact—and the resulting fear of getting hurt—can cause some kids to shy away from sports. Roughness can turn kids off, especially girls. The main emphasis of play should be fun. Inclusive fun. Creative fun. And yes, even aggressive fun—to a point.

Then: The wide-open grass fields had no boundaries and very few lines. Pat Dillon remembers just three circles—the two creases around each goal and one in the center for the draw. Streams, hillsides, and trees were the "natural" boundaries.

Now: Hard boundaries are right around the corner, according to Dillon. As lacrosse expands across the country and throughout the world, it's being played more and more often on AstroTurf fields ringed with tracks than on wide-open expanses of grass. Officially the playing area still is without uniform, measured boundaries, but visible guidelines—either solid or dashed to indicate the playing area—must be placed on all fields. The guidelines must be at least 4 meters from a change of surface, fence, or obstacle. A restraining line, implemented for safety's sake after a heated five-year debate, now limits the number of players on the offensive and defensive ends of the fields.

Questions and Answers

Q. What do you say to a parent who wants her daughter to wear a helmet and protective eyewear?

A. Hard helmets, such as bicycle helmets, are not approved for women's lacrosse. At the moment, no manufacturer makes soft headgear specifically for women's lacrosse.

Regarding eyewear, a player may wear an ASTM-approved (American Society for Testing and Materials) product.

Cherie Greer on Wooden Sticks

I think it's great for young players to learn using wooden sticks. Wood sticks help girls to learn the fundamentals. Girls just starting to play should try both. Then they can choose the kind of stick they like best. I prefer to use an STX wooden stick. I don't think the wooden stick is obsolete yet, although it might be moving in that direction. I might still switch, but I've been successful with the game using wood, so why fix something if it's not broken?

Cherie Greer, US Lacrosse national team member, U.S. World Cup team member for three championship teams (MVP, 1997 and 2001)

Cherie Greer, a three-time All-American, prefers to play with a traditional wooden lacrosse stick. Bill Welch

CHAPTER 2

Creating an Atmosphere of Good Habits

Winning: An Afterthought

Winning and success are not synonymous. Winning is nothing less than the unpredictable outcome of a contest. Success is nothing more than a good habit, or at least it can be. First, you and your team need to set individual and collective goals. Then, you put yourselves in situations in which you can work on accomplishing some of those goals.

Your team can enjoy many accomplishments, even in the face of a loss—if you teach them how; if your time and energy as a coach are spent pursuing success rather than just worrying about winning.

It might take some practice on your part—and some getting used to on the part of your players and their parents—to shift the focus off the score by emphasizing success in other aspects of the game. Here's a typical postgame perspective that you can try sharing with your girls: "Caroline was such a hustler after those ground balls! And Andrea's stick was a virtual vacuum cleaner, sucking up every pass within 10 yards. Jessica stuck to her player like bubble gum on a shoe, down on defense; and Molly's shots were hard and fast and confident, just like we practiced. And by the way, there's another thing I should mention: *we won*, 7 to 5!"

The philosophy of winning as an afterthought is not about being coy. It's about being a coach who cares more about players' spirits than game statistics. Simply put, it's about being a coach who cares. It can be difficult not to buy into the notion that you're successful only when you win. It's up to you to educate your co-coach, your players, and your parents just how skewed that notion is, and that the reality is you really win only when your team demonstrates success in the goals and objectives they set out to accomplish. Every game must have a winner and a loser. What's important is how the wins and the losses are perceived, reacted to, and emphasized. For many players, simply having the courage to participate is a measure of success. For others, success can be measured in terms of new and improved skills. Being on a team infinitely expands the definition of the word "win." Your players win every time they push themselves to learn something new about the game of lacrosse, or improve their athleticism and skills, or infect each other with the excitement of being involved with a team. They win every time they follow directions, exhibit confidence under pressure, and handle each other's unique personalities. They win when they come back for more after they thought they were spent, and when they deal gracefully with success as well as perceived failure. They win because their characters are, at least in part, being shaped and molded by you, their coach, whose main goal is to provide a fun environment where girls of various athletic abilities can learn a great sport and improve a little every day as athletes and individuals.

Promoting Good Habits

A big part of coaching is organizing and controlling group behavior and creating an atmosphere of good habits through positive energy and reinforcement.

The key to teaching kids to respond to your instructions and signals is to do it through fun activities. Good habits are actions that need to be consistently reinforced and practiced. As a coach, you're responsible for establishing a routine of behavior for every practice. Kids need and crave routine and ritual. The discipline of a routine will help establish your authority. It's the happily disciplined learning environment that leads to a positive sports experience: discipline via an energized approach to the habits, drills, and tactics that you're going to implement every practice.

Here are a helpful handful of good habits that will set your season off on the path of success.

Bring It In

You're strolling across a freshly mown field under a bluer-than-blue sky . . . OK, not really. But it's a nice fantasy. As we all know, youth lacrosse seasons start in the shivery month of March. In the mid-Atlantic states where we coach, the winter winds are still whipping under gray clouds. Whatever the weather, it's the least of your worries. What has you concerned, as you approach a group of eighteen eager lacrosse players, is the fact that they're all looking at you with fresh, expectant faces. You're probably thinking (even if you're a veteran coach): "What in the world am I doing here, with a girls' lacrosse stick in my left hand and a whistle in my right?"

There's nothing like a deep-cleansing breath, followed by a stout exhale into the whistle to calm your nerves and alleviate stage fright. One blast or two, that's up to your personal style. But never show up at practice without a whistle. It establishes authority; it sets you, the coach, apart from players and parents; and it attracts attention no matter how chatty or boisterous your group. Follow up the whistle with a short, definitive catch phrase. You might try calling, "Bring it in!"

Fantasy #2: The girls stop what they're doing to sprint toward you and wait in silence for you to impart your wisdom.

One or two girls actually might do that (they're just trying to butter you up so you choose them to play center), but most of the team is likely to take their time meandering over—chatting, swatting at grass bugs, and giggling—and gathering around you in a haphazard huddle.

Coach Tucker whistles "Let's bring it in!"

Face the Sun

You're the coach: the star of the show (at least for the time being). The spotlight's on you. You not only exude positive energy, but you also literally reflect it. Your face is bathed with light because you're facing the sun when you speak. It's not a matter of drama, but rather of practicality. You want to position yourself looking into the sun while in a huddle or during a demonstration so that your girls aren't squinting and distracted when you address them. You want their eyes locked on you. You want them concentrating on your words and actions.

These are two of the most elementary and important good habits you can establish right away, as a coach:

- wear a whistle and use it
- be aware of your environment (notably sun glare and wind) so that your players can comfortably focus on you

Bring It In, Again

A commitment to having fun while establishing good habits right from the beginning is the cornerstone of success for an entire season. The girls will respond best to your example of tending to the little things first. The bigger things may require more patience on your part, such as learning to bring it in quickly and enthusiastically. With the sun in your face, you might remark to your haphazard huddle, "Girls, that just wasn't good enough. That's not the attitude we want to have at our practices." They'll likely stare at you with blank faces.

That's when you need to explain that whenever you, the coach, blow a whistle and call "Bring it in!" you expect them to jog over to you enthusiastically and quickly and stand in front of you, without talking, ready to listen. Structure and consistency are key to maintaining control while having fun with a group that consists of varying skill levels.

You might say, "Everything we do is as a team, and as a team, we're going to bring it in better this time. Now, go back out there and try again!"

Instruct them to disperse and encourage them to really show their stuff when they bring it in this time. Then blow the whistle again. When the team gets it right, reinforce their behavior with enthusiasm, telling them that's what teamwork is all about, and have them acknowledge their success by high-fiving each other—as well as you—with their sticks. "That's the way to bring it in, girls! Great job. That's what I want to see before and after every practice!"

If there's a particularly shy or reticent player, make it a point to stand next to her in the huddle—perhaps asking her to hold your stick or even putting your arm around her—to help her focus and feel comfortable enough to listen to you instead of listening to the nay-saying that may be going on in her head.

Condition your players to respond to *huddle phrases* like "Girls, eyes on me!," "Listen up, girls!," and "Look over here, girls!" As you outline what the day's practice will be like, establish eye contact with each and every team member. Call each girl by name. Huddles need to be concise and precise. The attention span of young girls is short. An effective tactic is to single out those players who are listening well so the team knows this is a priority habit for you.

Coaches learn quickly how long (or short) their players' attention spans are. It's no secret that young players learn best by doing. Keep your comments short and to the point and get your players moving—doing drills or scrimmaging—as quickly as possible. No matter how trendy your girls are, remember this: kids with state-of-the-art sticks want the same things as we wooden-stick women did when we learned lacrosse thirty years ago. They want to improve, they want lots of action, and they want to have fun. These objectives will help guide you in the daily planning of practices and games. By fostering team unity and spirit, helping your players work cooperatively, and appreciating them as individuals, you'll earn the respect of your players and their parents. When you send them out of the huddle, make sure they leave just like they came: as a team.

Alex Is a Winner

Maryalice remembers 8-year-old Alex of her Tyker team from a couple of years ago. The team was in the midst of getting trounced in a tournament game. They hadn't scored a point. It was late in the game; there was no way they could win. Alex, like the rest of the team, still continued to give it her all: chasing down ground balls and defending with a vengeance. No one was more surprised than she was when her team assumed possession of the ball and completed a pretty series of passes, the third one landing in her stick. Maryalice yelled to her to go in to goal and shoot. She did, scoring for the very first time in a game in her fledgling lacrosse career. She promptly fell to her knees and commenced crying. Maryalice ran out on to the field, thinking Alex had hurt herself in the process of winging the shot into the goal. But no. Alex pulled herself up and clung to Maryalice while she continued to weep: "I'm just so happy!" she said, smiling through the tears.

Give a Shout

This good habit fosters enthusiasm and creates an energized atmosphere. Giving a shout can be a comfortable ritual that sets the tone at the beginning and end of every practice. Shouting together in a boisterous way promotes team unity and togetherness.

Some shout-worthy suggestions: "Together!," "Teamwork!," "Energy!," "Ground balls!," "Dynamite (substitute your team's name)!" Have all the girls gather in a tight circle, sticks facing inside, all together. Then, give a shout!

High-fives all around!

Hey, You!

We saved our favorite good habit for last. Your players—probably a mix of your own children, your friends' children, neighborhood kids, and a smattering of unknowns—need to be comfortable in addressing you. That means you need to tell them how to do it. Whatever you decide you want to be called—"Coach," or a nickname, or your first or last name—make sure to keep it consistent. ("Coach Yakutchik" was a bit much for Maryalice's first Tyker team to wrap their 6-year-old tongues around, so she became known as Coach Mary. Janine, who wasn't many years older than the players she coached when she first began coaching at Johns Hopkins, thought it best to more formally establish her authority as Coach Tucker.)

When you introduce yourself, you might tell your players when and where you played, if you did. If you didn't play, lie (just kidding); assure them that you learned everything you need to know about lacrosse in your handy-dandy *Baffled Parent's Guide*! This is probably as good a moment as any to set up a one-time-a-season exercise that we call Trust Me.

A coach needs, first and foremost, to establish trust. Respect will follow. In this exercise, not only will you establish yourself as a capable (and fun) leader, but you'll also build a foundation for the all-important coach-player rapport, something that will deepen throughout the season as you get to know each other better.

Ask your players to stand in a line, about an arm's length apart, facing away from you. Ask them to close their eyes. Explain that, one at a time, when you are behind them and give the signal, they should fall backward, and you will catch them. (*Note:* The effectiveness of this exercise is inversely related to the number of players you drop—so don't drop anyone!)

Position yourself a couple of feet behind the first player, at arm's length. With your arms extended, encourage the player to fall backward. As the player drops backward, grasp her under her arms and bend your knees as she falls into your grip. Take a small step backward as her weight falls into you, giving with her momentum. Amid the nervous giggles and occasional screams of delight, you'll establish a bond of trust and belief in your abilities as a coach who cares about each individual as well as the team as a whole.

Questions and Answers

Q. I have a player who's consistently late for practices and another who regularly leaves early for another activity. How should I address these disruptions?

A. Part of the privilege of playing on a team is respecting the other players on it and the rules the coach has established. At the initial meeting with parents and players, one of your expectations should be the importance of starting practice on time and staying until its conclusion. However, you're bound to have at least some players involved in multi-

Dee Fichter Cross on Her Favorite Coach

My favorite lacrosse coach was Sue Kidder, my coach at Norristown Area High School in Pennsylvania in 1977. She had a way of challenging us and making it fun, too. She always believed in us as a team and never gave up, even though we never won even one game. That was amazing. She was such a talented player, having played on the U.S. team, and she never once looked down on us because we weren't as talented. I really appreciated that.

Dee Fichter Cross, two-time U.S. World Cup team member, former high school lacrosse coach, current coach of her daughters' youth lacrosse program

ple activities that conflict with your schedule. We've found the best way to address these issues is to communicate directly with the parents, because lateness often isn't a player's fault. If family commitments, work schedules, or other conflicts are making it difficult for them to be punctual, try to help arrange another way for the player to get to practice, maybe with another teammate. Encourage carpooling—it can build friendships and camaraderie.

Q. I have a couple of players who consistently talk when I'm talking. It distracts me and the other team members. How do I handle this?

A. This is disrespectful behavior, and it shouldn't be tolerated. Simply say, "Excuse me," to the player who is being disruptive and remind her that one of the team rules is to respect the rights of others. Usually this is enough. If the disruptive player continues to talk, let her know this isn't acceptable by calmly asking her to remove herself from the huddle and sit quietly on the sideline. Before beginning the next activity, take the player aside, encourage her to follow the team rules, and ask her to rejoin the team. If the negative behavior continues, you should have a meeting with the player and her parents to discuss a solution to the problem.

Q. Some of my more highly skilled players are beginning to criticize those who are less skilled. What do I do about it?

A. Tell your players and parents in the beginning of the season that one golden rule of your team is that the coach does the critiquing and correcting of players. Period. The players and parents are expected to be 100 percent supportive of all team members in order to foster unity and spirit. Player-to-player criticism chips away at the foundation of what it means to be a team. Any time during the season is a good time to remind everyone of this rule.

CHAPTER 3

Before Hitting the Field: Girls' Lacrosse in a Nutshell

Lacrosse is known as the fastest game on two feet. The girls' game is characterized by exciting fast breaks and fluid passing series from one end of the field to the goal, as well as settled offensive and defensive play. This chapter will familiarize you with the field, the equipment, and the basic rules of the game.

Overview

Everyone who's involved with girls' lacrosse—coaches, parents, umpires, fans, and, of course, players—needs to familiarize themselves each season with the latest rules and levels of play sanctioned by US Lacrosse, the national governing body of lacrosse. The rules referred to in this book are taken directly from the section on girls' lacrosse in the latest rule book from US Lacrosse (*Women's Rules 2003: Official Rules for Girls & Women's Lacrosse*; see the resources section for US Lacrosse contact information). The rules are "designed to maintain the spirit of the game and to ensure the safety of the players at all levels." Youth leagues may decide on age-level play that best suits their needs within the following suggested guidelines: 6 to 8 years old (Under 9); 9 to 10 years old (Under 11); and 11 to 12 years old (Under 13).

Three levels of play (A, B, and C) are recognized, depending on the experience of the players. Rules for Levels B and C are appropriate for beginning players: no checking is allowed, and sticks may be modified to make throwing and catching easier. Level A rules allow modified checking and require regulation sticks and pockets.

Level A specifics:

- eleven field players, one goalie
- recommended field size is 100 yards by 70 yards
- regular field markings, including restraining line

- regular women's sticks, regulation pockets
- modified checking only
- 25-minute halves (maximum) running time
- may shoot from direct free positions (see pages 32–33)

Level B specifics:

- eleven field players, one goalie
- recommended field size is 90 yards by 50 yards
- regular field markings, including restraining line
- regular women's sticks, modified pockets allowed
- no checking
- 25-minute halves (maximum) running time
- may shoot from direct free positions

Level C specifics:

- seven field players, a goalie is optional
- recommended field size is 50 yards by 25 yards
- field markings include an 8-meter arc but no 12-meter fan, no restraining line, and a centerline but no circle
- youth sticks (mesh allowed) or regular women's sticks, modified pockets allowed
- no checking
- 20-minute halves (maximum) running time
- may not shoot from any free position

The Field

One thing that makes girls' lacrosse unique is that the playing area has no uniformly measured boundaries. This no-hard-boundaries concept hails back to the days when Native Americans played the sport over miles and miles of their territory. However, years of heated debate about this issue seem to have paved the way for hard-line boundaries; although not instituted yet, they could be just around the corner. Until then, the guidelines (measured in U.S. and metric units) used to mark a women's lacrosse field consist of two *goal lines* that are no more than 100 yards apart and no less than 90 yards apart. There must be at least 13 and no more than 20 yards of space behind each goal line running the width of the field. The field should have no less than 60 and no more than 70 yards of playable width.

Visible guidelines (either solid or dashed) must be placed on the *sidelines* and the *end lines* and must be at least 4 meters from a change of surface, fence, or obstacle. On fields where dashed lines are used, they should measure 2 meters (6 feet, 6 inches) in length and five such lines should be placed: along each sideline; one at each end line; one at each restraining line, and one at the center. Two dashed lines should be placed behind each goal. There is a *center circle* with a 3-meter (9 feet, 11 inches) line in the middle—the *centerline*—parallel to the goal lines. If extended, the centerline would represent the 50-yard line. This is where the *center draw* takes place to start each game, to restart the game after goals, and to start the second half. On either end of the field a solid line extends across the width of the field, 30 yards from the goal line, and is called the *restraining line*. The restraining line must be clearly distinguishable, as it limits the number of players that can be in the offensive or defensive end at one time. On each end of the field is a *crease*, or *goal circle*, that measures 8½ feet from the center of the goal line and surrounds the *goal cage*, which measures 6-by-6 feet. An *8-meter arc* and a *12-meter fan* extend out from each crease and are used when fouls occur. A *critical scoring area*, an unmarked area of the field about 15 yards in diameter and 10 yards behind the goal circle, is used to evaluate shooting space and the setup for free positions on certain fouls. The *goal line extended* is an imaginary extension of the goal line used as a reference for defenders and attackers when executing moves on the field. The illustrations (below and next page) show the correct terminology and measurements for a girls' lacrosse field.

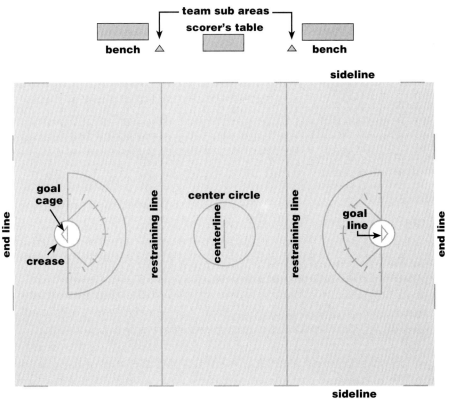

Field terminology.

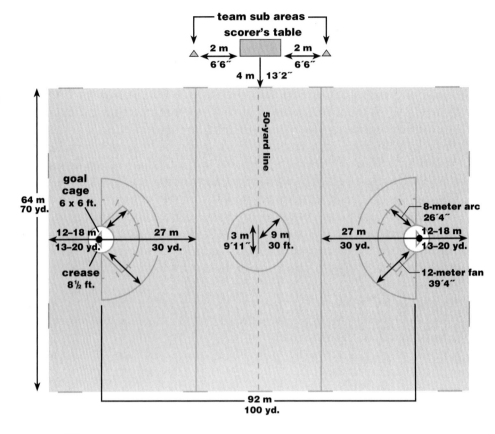

Field dimensions.

The Ball

A lacrosse ball is made of solid rubber, is slightly smaller than a tennis ball, weighs about 5 ounces, and comes in a variety of colors. At the high school and collegiate levels, girls are required to play with a yellow ball (boys play with a white ball). We recommend staying consistent with the higher levels and using yellow balls for your girls' practices and games.

Equipment
Sticks

Girls' lacrosse sticks—usually made of wood or plastic—consist of a head, neck, shaft, pocket, sidewall, throwing strings, and sidewall strings. Plastic sticks are the most popular among today's players, probably because they're light, aerodynamic, and flexible. There are a number of different styles to choose from. The shapes of the stick heads vary widely; some promise advantages such as greater ball control, a quicker release of the ball, a deeper pocket, and a greater ease of picking up a ground ball.

The plastic *head* of the stick is screwed onto the *shaft* or handle at the *neck*. The *ball stopper* is the foam pad at the bottom of the stick head used to cushion the ball as it rests in the pocket. Stick shafts can be made of aluminum, titanium, wood, or a composite material. Stick heads can have *open* or *closed sidewalls* for greater or less flexibility. Most sticks today have at least a partially open sidewall. The *pocket* of a wooden stick is strung with vertical thongs of leather or synthetic material and woven in a crisscross pattern with gut or nylon strings. The pocket of a plastic stick head is strung with vertical thongs of leather or synthetic material and cross-woven with nylon strings. In the girls' game, only the goalie's stick can be strung with a mesh pocket, with one exception: Youth Level C rules allow field players to use mesh pocket sticks. We recommend familiarizing young players with regulation women's lacrosse sticks as soon as possible. You might slightly modify the pockets to make throwing and catching a bit easier, but the sooner your girls get used to regulation sticks the better!

The pocket. A girls' lacrosse stick is considered legal if the top of the ball is even with or above the plastic or wooden walls of the stick head. Sticks are designed today with smaller sidewalls that allow for deeper pockets and thus greater throwing velocity and accuracy. However, the smaller sidewalls may offer less protection for the ball. Before a game begins, the umpire will check each player's stick to make sure the pocket is legal. A player with an illegal pocket will be asked to tighten her pocket and have it checked again before she is able to take the field. In Youth Level C rules, players may use a youth stick with mesh or traditional stringing or a regulation women's lacrosse stick with a modified pocket. A *modified pocket* allows half the ball to fall below the bottom of the sidewall. Level B players must use a regular women's lacrosse stick with either a modified or a regulation pocket. Level A players must use a regulation women's lacrosse stick with a regular, legal pocket.

Stick length. Girls' and women's lacrosse sticks must be between 35½ and 43¼ inches long. Younger players (ages 6 to 10) may play with shorter sticks (about arm's length), but we recommend getting regulation-length sticks into the hands of young players as soon as possible. A goalie stick should measure between 35½ and 48 inches long and can be strung traditionally, with leather and nylon, or with mesh. The head of a goalie stick is much larger than that of a field player's stick, measuring 13 by 16½ inches.

A state-of-the-art regulation women's lacrosse stick with a legal pocket.

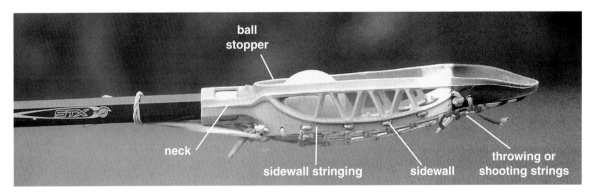

ball stopper

neck

sidewall stringing

sidewall

throwing or shooting strings

Defenders might prefer slightly longer sticks and attackers slightly shorter ones. The standard way to determine a comfortable shaft length is to extend the arm, gripping the stick below the stick head at the shaft; where the bottom of the stick meets the shoulder is generally the proper length for the player. Defensive players might want more length for reach, and offensive players might like shorter shafts so they can protect their sticks better. If bothersome lengths of leather thongs extend below the head of the stick and tend to flap (these are used to tighten or loosen the pocket), suggest your girls use colored tape to affix them, or help the girls braid or cut the leather thongs. It's the little things that make a cool, customized stick.

We strongly encourage players to hold the stick with their top hand placed about one-third of the way down the stick (give or take an inch or two in either direction). Wrap a colorful piece of athletic tape about a third of the way down the stick as a reminder for the top-hand position for routine cradling and catching. You don't want your players choked up with death grips at the tops of the sticks. The bottom hand should be positioned at the bottom of the stick as the anchor. The pinkie goes underneath the base, with the butt of the stick resting on the inside of the pinkie to allow for greater control.

Place a second piece of tape about two-thirds of the way down the stick (give or take an inch or two) to indicate where a girl should hold the stick while playing defense. Note that the top hand slides farther down the shaft on defense than attack to allow for greater reach.

Mouth Guards

It is extremely important to enforce the rule that *all* players must wear mouth guards not only during games but also at practices. There are a number of different kinds of over-the-counter mouth guards that can be molded to fit comfortably. Many players choose to get custom-fitted mouth guards from their family dentist. We recommend that youth coaches keep a supply of spare mouth guards in their equipment bags at all times. Field players may also choose to wear close-fitting gloves, soft headgear, and eye protection or safety goggles that meet American Society for Testing and Materials (ASTM) standards for girls' and women's lacrosse. This equipment is optional, although eye protection is beginning to be required in some areas of the country at upper levels of play.

Shoes

Special lacrosse shoes are not required. Some girls choose to wear cleats while others wear running shoes. Many major shoe manufacturers offer multiple choices in appropriate footwear for lacrosse.

Gloves

Women's lacrosse gloves are optional, but if desired can be purchased at any major sporting goods store.

Goalie Equipment

Goalies must wear the following protective equipment: a helmet with a face mask, a separate throat protector, a mouthpiece, and a chest protector. At the youth level, goalies *must* wear leg padding on the shins and thighs. Protection for the abdominal area is strongly recommended as well. If desired, goalies may wear additional padding on their hands, arms, shoulders, and shins as long as it is close-fitting and not more than an inch thick. For more on goalies, see chapter 13.

Players and Positions

A girls' lacrosse team generally consists of eighteen to twenty-two players. Seven to eleven players are on the field at one time (depending on the age and level of the players) plus goalies. The remaining team members, waiting their turn on the sidelines, are support players. (We don't like the term "substitutes," which can have a negative connotation.) A twelve-player team consists of one goalie, four defenders, three midfielders, and four attackers. Traditionally, the position names for the defenders are point, cover point, and third man. The traditional names for attackers are first home, second home, and third home, and the midfielders consist of two defense wings, two attack wings, and a center. With the introduction of the restraining line a few years ago, many teams now refer to the positions as goalie, four defenders, three midfielders, and four attackers to allow the players flexibility to cover more areas on the field. Traditionally, for example, first homes rarely left the area

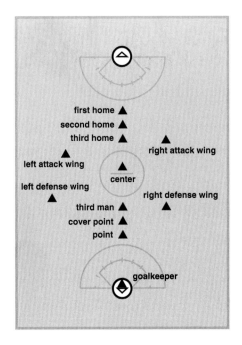

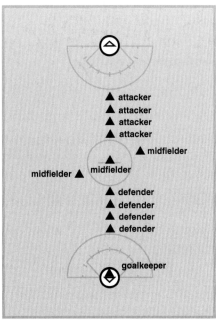

Left: Traditional player positions were more specific.

Right: Current player positions, as in the men's game, are more general.

around the goal. But today's attackers are encouraged to interchange their positions on the field, playing to the opposite 30-yard line when the opponent has the ball and going over on defense if the situation presents itself.

The *goalie* is the player responsible for stopping opponents' shots. She is also the player who will begin the transition from defense to offense after she makes a save.

The *defenders* help the goalie by defending opponents in the *critical scoring area*, or the area slightly larger than the 12-meter fan in front of the goal that includes a 10-yard area behind the goal. When playing player-to-player defense, each defender is assigned to an opposing attacker.

The *midfielders* are responsible not only for defending their goal area but also for helping on the offensive end of the field. These versatile players do the most running during games because they're responsible for playing the whole field. The attackers and defenders generally stay on their offensive and defensive ends of the field; however, they *are* allowed to move over the restraining line into the opposite end of the field. Any four players can stay back behind the restraining line to avoid the offside foul.

The *attackers* generally stay in their team's offensive half of the field. They set up the scoring opportunities and assist the midfielders in transitioning the ball into the offensive end of the field. However, attackers do have defensive responsibilities. When the other team's goalie makes a save, the attackers are expected to *ride* or pressure the defenders so they can't easily clear the ball out of the defensive end. A ride in lacrosse is like a full-court press in basketball.

Support players should be called on regularly, especially for the midfield positions, where players do lots of running. The more experience that support players get, the faster they will develop their game sense and skills.

Length of Game

The running times of girls' lacrosse games vary with the levels of play. Games for Levels A and B have a maximum of 25 minutes running time per half. Level C games have a maximum of 20 minutes running time per half. At every level, the game clock runs continuously, stopping after whistles only in the last 2 minutes of each half. The umpire can also stop the clock for an injury or emergency. Before each game, the coaches or team captains determine how long the halftime break will be, up to but not exceeding 10 minutes.

Scoring

Each goal equals one point. The team scoring the most goals is the winner. A goal is scored when the entire ball passes completely over the goal line, in between the goal posts, and under the crossbar from in front of the goal cage. The ball must be propelled from an attacker's stick or can be deflected off a defender's or goalie's stick or body.

Getting Started

The Center Draw

A center draw takes place at the midfield on the centerline and is used to start each half of a game and any overtime periods. After a goal is scored, the game is restarted with a center draw at the centerline. However, girls' youth lacrosse rules state that a free position will be taken at the centerline by the team with fewer goals if a four-or-more-goal differential exists.

The umpire sets up the center draw. A midfield player from each team stands with one foot toeing the center line and in a position to propel the ball into her offensive end of the field. Since there are a number of ways to take the center draw, remind players who take the draw always to have the backs of their sticks facing their goal cage.

Midfielders arranged around the center circle, anticipating the draw.

During the draw, only five players from each team may be in the midfield area between the restraining lines. Those players positioned around the center circle must have their feet *outside* the center circle until the whistle blows. All remaining players must be positioned outside the restraining lines. All players, with the exception of the two centers, are allowed to move while the draw is being taken, so long as they don't cross into the center circle or step over the restraining line until the whistle blows. During draws, encourage your players to move around the outside of the center circle. This can help them get a step on defenders, establish better angles to the ball, or box out defenders.

Top: Two opponents set up a center draw to start the game.

Bottom: The ball flies up, up, and away on a picture-perfect center draw.

The sticks of the pair of players taking the draw are placed back to back, with the back of each stick facing its player's goal. The bottom rims of the stick are in line with each other, slightly above hip level, parallel to the centerline and directly above it. The umpire places the ball in between the stick heads as they are held back to back. In order for the ball to stay put until the whistle, the players taking the center draw must keep their sticks aligned together. The umpire says "Ready" to signal the players taking the draw. They must remain motionless until they hear the whistle. On the whistle, the two players pull their sticks up and away from one another's. This motion should send the ball into the air. In order for a draw to be legal, the ball must be propelled higher than the heads of the players taking the draw. A free position is given to the opponent in the event of an illegal draw. The player who drew illegally is placed 4 meters (4.4 yards) away from the ball carrier to either side at a 45-degree angle from the centerline and toward the goal she is defending. If both players draw illegally, a throw is awarded.

A *throw* is used when both players draw illegally or when it can't be determined why the draw was illegal. A throw is also used when two players are equally close to the ball as it goes out of bounds, or when two players commit offsetting fouls. The umpire positions two players at least 1 meter (1.1 yards) apart, with the defensive player closest to the goal she is defending. The umpire tosses the ball in between the two players, who move onto the ball and try to catch it in the air. Teach your players to try to get a step ahead of their opponents during the throw (to cut off an opponent's angle to the ball) and to extend their sticks as far as possible to get to the ball first.

Out-of-Bounds

Because there are no uniform measured boundaries in girls' lacrosse, the player closest to the ball when it goes out of the playing area is awarded the ball. Teach your players to run hard after the ball as it is going out of the playing area and not to stop until they hear the umpire's whistle. An emphasis on hustle will promote aggressive pursuit of the ball and will win your team critical possessions. The player closest to the ball is brought onto the field 4 meters from the boundary and must be given 1 meter of playing space. Play continues on the umpire's whistle.

Stand on the Whistle

All play starts and stops with the umpire's whistle. All players must stop and stand still when the whistle blows to stop play. All players may move again when the next whistle blows to start play.

Substitution

In girls' lacrosse, substitution is unlimited. A team may substitute any time during play, after goals are scored, and at halftime. Multiple substitutions are allowed, but we recommend substituting one player at a time. A player who was substituted may reenter the game as soon as and as often as needed. Players must substitute through the team substitution area, which is by the scorer's table (if you have one). The player coming off the field must completely exit the field before her substitute may run onto the field. This applies to every position on the field.

Fouls

We recommend purchasing the latest rule book from US Lacrosse (*Women's Rules 2003: Official Rules for Girls & Women's Lacrosse*; see the resources section for US Lacrosse contact information). Girls' youth lacrosse programs adhere to these rules; there is a separate section dedicated to youth rules and regulations. Penalties are assessed differently, depending on how serious a foul is and where it occurs on the field. Fouls in the midfield are penalized differently from fouls in the critical scoring area. Listed below are some of the main rule infractions in the girls' game.

Major Fouls

Major fouls are called when the stick or body is used in a potentially dangerous way. Players may not use their sticks in an intimidating or reckless manner. They may not recklessly check another player's stick or swing their stick toward the body or head of an opponent. A player may not position her stick to *hold* an opponent's stick or body, impeding progress. Attackers may not hold or cradle the ball in their stick directly in front of their faces.

A number of major fouls involve misuse of the body. A player may not block her opponent by moving into her path without giving her a chance to stop or change direction. Girls may not push or detain opponents. The ball carrier may not charge into another player, lean into an opponent with her shoulder, or back into an opponent. Girls may not set illegal *picks* in which body contact occurs—picks that don't allow time or space for the opponent

An umpire calls blocking—
a defensive foul—using her
yellow flag.

to stop or change direction. (For more on picks, see pages 70–71.) Tripping is illegal. Players may not *false-start*, or move before the whistle starts play.

There are also major fouls that occur only in the critical scoring area. For example, a defender may not be in the 8-meter arc for more than 3 seconds without actively marking an opponent. The defender must be within a stick's length of her opponent to avoid being in violation of this 3-second rule. Obstruction of shooting space is another major foul in the critical scoring area. *Shooting space* is the cone-shaped space extending from the ball carrier to the outside of the goal circle. A defender who is not within a stick's length of her attack player may not block the *free space to goal* when an attacker is looking to shoot or in the act of shooting. Offensive players may not take dangerous or uncontrolled shots and may not follow through with their sticks in a dangerous manner. Offensive players may not shoot directly at a field player or intentionally at the goalie.

Direct Free Positions

When a major foul is committed in the midfield, the opposing team is awarded a direct free position where the foul occurred. The player who committed the foul is positioned 4 meters behind the fouled player.

If the foul occurs in the 8-meter arc, the attacker is positioned on the closest hash mark on the 8-meter arc, and the defender who committed the foul is placed 4 meters behind, on the 12-meter fan. The umpire clears the arc, as well as the penalty lane, and all players must exit the 8-meter arc toward the closest 8-meter line. This allows for a safe execution of the penalty near the goal. On the umpire's whistle, the player with the ball may shoot, pass, or maintain possession of the ball.

If a foul is committed inside the 8-meter arc by the attacking team, the defense will be awarded the ball on the 8-meter arc and the attacker who fouled must go 4 meters behind. All remaining players must be 4 meters away from the ball carrier. Again, play starts on the umpire's whistle.

Minor Fouls

Because minor fouls do not involve dangerous play or interrupt play, the penalties are less severe. Players may not cover a ground ball with their stick or guard it with their feet. Girls may not check empty sticks. Players may not *ward off* opponents with a free hand or arm. Field players may not touch the ball with their hand, use their body to keep the ball in the stick, or use their body to play the ball. Players may not wear jewelry in a game, intentionally delay the game (for example, by not wearing a mouthpiece), or deliberately cause the ball to go out-of-bounds. An indirect free position is awarded where the foul occurred for a minor foul, but the fouling player is moved 4 meters away from the fouled player in the direction from which she approached when she committed the foul. Play restarts on the umpire's whistle.

Indirect Free Position

An indirect free position is awarded for minor fouls by the defense that occur inside the 12-meter fan. The player who committed the foul is moved 4 meters away. The player who was fouled may not take a shot on goal; she must pass the ball to a teammate who then can shoot on goal.

Fouls around the Crease

A number of rules govern play around the crease, or goal circle. For example, a field player may not enter the crease, or have any part of her body or stick in the crease at any time unless she is *deputizing* or standing in for the goalie (who has moved out of the crease). Neither the goalie nor her deputy may hold the ball for more than 10 seconds inside the crease. They may not, while inside the crease, play the ball in the air or on the ground with their hand if the ball is outside of the crease. If the goalie steps outside of the crease she may not *rake* or draw the ball into her goal circle. Once outside the crease, she may not step back in while in possession of the ball. If a defender runs into the crease, a minor foul is committed, and the attacking team will be awarded an indirect free position on the 12-meter fan out to either side of the goal and level with the goal line. If an attacker runs into the crease or her stick crosses into the crease, a minor foul is committed and the goalie is awarded the ball inside the goal circle.

Erin Brown on Her Favorite Coaches

My favorite coaches were my high school coach, Sue Strobel, and my U.S. team coach, Sue Stahl. Coach Strobel was completely invested in the philosophy of having her players be multidimensional. Coach Stahl's gift was to instill in me the grace of the game.

Erin Brown, U.S. World Cup team member,
Director, Women's Division, US Lacrosse

Team Fouls

A team may not have more than seven players over the restraining line in their offensive end of the field. Subsequently, a team may not have more than eight players (which includes the goalie) over the restraining line in their defensive end of the field. In both cases, this would be an offside foul. Players may exchange places during play, but it's important that the player has both feet over the line before a teammate can cross the restraining line. If any part of the foot is over the restraining line, the player is in violation. When a ball is rolling toward the restraining line, a player may reach over the line with her stick to play the ball, as long as no part of her foot crosses the line.

Umpires

At the youth level, it's strongly recommended by US Lacrosse that at least one qualified umpire be assigned to Level C games, and two qualified umpires be assigned to games for Levels A and B. It is the umpire's job to enforce safety and fairness in the game. The umpire carries a whistle, a yellow flag, and a set of green, yellow, and red cards that are used to control the play and safety of the game. We strongly recommend that coaches and umpires recognize the fact that their collective mission is to keep the game safe and fun for all players. We are all on the same team, in that sense. "Civilized" interaction between coaches and umpires is encouraged by Pat Dillon, Rules Chair of the Women's Division of US Lacrosse. The official should greet both coaches, setting a cordial and friendly tone, and vice versa. Umpires as well as coaches should carry a copy of the rule book in their game bags. Youth umpires should be focused on teaching as they call games, Dillon says. Remember, umpires are setting an example for the 6- to 12-year-old players in their care. They should be willing to take the time to explain themselves to coaches and players when approached in a calm and rational way.

CHAPTER 4

Setting Up the Season

One of the most daunting challenges facing a new coach is organizing the many facets of a season: figuring how many practices to have in a week and deciding when and where to have them; how to get uniforms; who is responsible for equipment; how to contact everyone if a practice is canceled—the list of details goes on and on. The best defense against being sucked under by administrative quicksand is a good offense: plan your season ahead of time.

Our strategy for an ideal season schedule is to try to hold practices twice a week and games once a week. This allows players to improve their skills and learn team systems and strategies but usually doesn't overburden already busy families.

The coach, umpire, and players discuss youth rule changes. Maryalice Yakutchik

Details, Details

Priority #1: Find out the name and phone number of a point person, whether it's a school administrator or the commissioner of a recreational league lacrosse program. Whoever your liaison is should help guide you in terms of field availability, roster of players, recommendations for assistant coaches, setting up your game and practice schedule, ordering of uniforms, and contact information for officials and other coaches.

A Coach's Equipment Checklist

whistle	extra mouth guards
women's lacrosse stick	first-aid kit and ice pack
clipboard with daily practice plan and pen	12 small, flat plastic cones
team roster	baby powder or white spray paint for touching up
reversible jerseys or pinnies	lines on the field
ball bag with at least three dozen balls	access to a cell phone for emergencies

Once you have the bare bones of your season—the roster, the phone numbers of players, and practice days, times, and sites—you're ready to contact your team.

Rope 'Em In

The initial phone calls to your team members and their parents will serve several purposes. First, you'll introduce yourself and welcome them to your team. Next, you want to share with them a brief practice and game schedule: "Hey, we'll be practicing on Tuesdays and Thursdays at the middle school from 4 to 5:30 P.M., and our games will usually be on Saturday mornings." Next, tell them there will be a parent meeting after the first practice—just for 10 minutes or so—and stress mandatory attendance.

Last of all, hit them with the zinger: "Do you have any background in girls' lacrosse, and/or would you be interested in being involved with the team?" Keep in mind that the most important quality of a helper-assistant is a positive, friendly manner. You want someone who interacts well with you, your players, and parents and who treats everyone with respect. You can offer a range of responsibilities for volunteers to pick and choose. For instance, you'll need someone to volunteer to set up a phone tree for bad weather or canceled practices; someone to handle uniform distribution and collection; someone to organize team dinners or tailgates; a few folks to be team moms or dads who arrange halftime snacks and drinks for game days; and as many volunteers as possible to assist with travel arrangements for away games, such as distributing directions and organizing car pools if necessary. Avoid dictating the responsibilities. Allow parents to have ownership in the decision-making process.

Having assistant coaches allows you to teach different skills at the same time or the same skills to players with varying levels of ability. You'll need at least one—preferably two—assistant coaches. You'll need a dependable assistant—or assistants—who will commit to consistently attending practices and games. They're your meat-and-potatoes people, your staples. You might also try finding a local college or high school player—an older sister or babysitter of one of your girls can be a great resource. She'll be the one who ultimately will end up having celebrity status on your team; invite her to show up whenever her schedule allows. She'll no doubt inject enthusiasm and new ideas into your practices.

The more assistants you can rope in, the better off you and your team will be. Perhaps one way to expand your pool is to offer parents "flextime": if someone can come only once a week or even once every other week, take it.

Ideally, your assistant coaches reflect and complement the philosophies, energy, and expectations of the head coach. Make it clear from the beginning that you expect your assistants to be fair, upbeat, and energetic when interacting with players, parents, fellow coaches, and umpires. Each coach will have his or her own personality and style; that's a good thing. It doesn't matter whether your coaches' natures are tough or soft, as long as their words and actions are constructive, not destructive.

Hopefully, your initial introductory phone calls will yield, at the very least, an able assistant for your first practice.

Of course, you'll encounter parents who don't want to be involved, or can't be, and that's OK. It's out of your control. Your job is to let all parents know that help and support is needed and would be appreciated. In fact, some parents may be downright disagreeable about your practice schedule or any number of issues. Here's a heads-up: being a coach of a girls' youth lacrosse team is not all smooth sailing. Parents will complain about practice schedules, and girls will whine about playing time. Stick to your guns. Gently remind them that you're a volunteer doing your best to ensure a fun season for all, and remind them that that will happen only if "we all play nice together in the sandbox." Keep the lines of communication open and consistent. Whenever you communicate with parents, always maintain emotional control. Have a sense of humor; it goes a long way in disarming people. Let them know it's OK to disagree, but everyone involved deserves to be treated with respect.

Before you end your initial phone call, remind parents that they'll be asked to stay after the first practice for a few minutes to fill out a questionnaire.

Set the Ground Rules

When you meet the parents at the meeting after the first practice, keep it short and establish your style as a coach and your expectations for the season before the season starts. For instance, you might introduce yourself and tell a bit about your experiences as a player and coach. Explain your general phi-

---

Preseason Questionnaire for Parents

Player's Name: _____

Health Issues/Allergies: _____

Parent's Names and Occupations: _____

_____

Home Address/Phone Number: _____

_____

Work Phone: _____

E-mail Address: _____

Emergency Contact—name and phone number: _____

_____

Player Profile—years of experience, name of program, preferred position: _____

Parent Profile—previous lacrosse experience, playing or coaching: _____

Extended Family Profile—lacrosse experience: _____

Are you interested in volunteering in the program? _____

In what capacity can you best help? _____

---

losophy: the girls are here to have a positive sports experience that involves fun, learning, playing in the spirit of the game, and observing rules. Then get specific about how your philosophy will dictate playing time, game etiquette, and positions. Here are some guidelines.

Playing time: Every girl will play at least 40 percent of the game (check to see if your recreational council has other guidelines that you're required to follow).

Game etiquette: Coaches coach; spectators cheer. There will be zero tolerance for yelling at officials or criticizing players.

Positions: We recommend that players have an opportunity to try a range of positions on the field at the youth level. Express to your team members and parents that there will be opportunities throughout the season for each of them to develop as "complete" lacrosse players—meaning that an offensive player develops defensive skills, and a defensive player develops offensive skills. Avoid the pigeonholing of young players.

Equipment: Tell your parents when and where uniforms will be

Sample Preseason Letter to Parents

Dear Lacrosse Parents,

I'm excited for the spring lacrosse season and am looking forward to working with you and coaching your girls. Let's all come together with energy and enthusiasm to benefit our children.

My goal for the season is for each girl to have fun while improving her lacrosse skills. My philosophy is to foster a positive, supportive atmosphere so that every player has a great experience. Regardless of ability, every member of the team will see playing time and be treated with encouragement and respect by the coaching staff.

I look to you to help me reinforce several important concepts that embody the spirit of sport and teamwork. You can do this by arriving at practices and games on time; treating officials, team members, and coaches with respect; cheering enthusiastically from the sidelines; and keeping in mind that success means showing improvement, not necessarily winning.

Games: Please arrive 30 minutes before the scheduled start. If you know that getting your child to a game will be difficult, please make carpooling arrangements. If your child can't make it to a game, please let me know in advance. If she misses practice the week before the game, she may not see as much playing time in the game as others who did attend. Please understand I have this policy so that participation in the games is fair to everyone.

Cancellation: Unless you hear otherwise, we'll have practice at the middle school on Tuesdays and Thursdays from 4 to 5:30 P.M., and games will be scheduled on Saturday mornings. In case of cancellation because of weather or unforeseen circumstances, you'll be notified by means of a phone tree that will be set up and sent home shortly.

Equipment needs are mercifully minimal: a mouth guard, lacrosse stick, water bottle, and appropriate shoes. Gloves are optional. All personal equipment should be labeled with her name. Make sure girls with long hair have the means to pull it back off their faces. Jewelry is prohibited during practices and games.

We're looking forward to a great season of lacrosse. If you have any questions or concerns, don't hesitate to contact me.

Thanks,
The Coach
123 Main Street
222-3333
coach@lacrosse.com

Danielle Gallagher on Her Favorite Coach

Feffie Barnhill, former coach at the College of William and Mary, enabled me to take my game to the next level. She taught me how to draw from my experiences on the basketball court and apply them to the lacrosse field. She also taught me how to be competitive and that the most important part is to have fun and enjoy playing.

Danielle Gallagher, U.S. World Cup team member

---

distributed and how to deal with issues about size. Ideally, a girl's uniform consists of a numbered league T-shirt and shorts. In most programs, players are expected to provide their own stick, mouth guard, gloves, shoes, and water bottle.

Save 5 minutes at the end of the meeting to elicit parent feedback. Tell them that you'll likely be available before and after most practices, and if they have any concerns or comments, that you'd appreciate them talking to you directly. Emphasize that open communication is key for everyone to have a great season. Hand out the preseason letter. (If any parents can't attend the meeting, make sure to mail them a copy.)

Questions and Answers

Q. Our facilities are limited and our team was allotted only one night a week to practice. Is this enough?

A. No. Players need to acquire skills and concepts through repetition. Practicing only once a week will affect your players' recall and won't allow you to move forward as quickly as you'd like. You can look into other practice sites. You don't need a regulation field or even goals to accomplish lots of skill work with your players. Ask your team parents if they know of any fields or large yards within the community that could serve as possible practice sites. An alternative might be to approach a coach of another team in the same age group that practices on a different night and suggest sharing the field so both of you have two nights of practice a week. You'll still run your own practice on your half of the field, plus you'll have the opportunity to enhance your practice with a scrimmage against the other team. Remember, kids love to play.

CHAPTER 5

Essential Skills: A Progressive Approach

Cradling, throwing, catching, and picking up ground balls: these are some of the fundamental skills of girls' lacrosse. This chapter describes these basic skills in a way that can be easily taught to your players. And it touches on some not-so-basic skills, too—such as putting a spin on an ordinary bounce shot. By the way, never say to yourself, "My players aren't good enough to try such fancy maneuvers," or "My players are too young to be taught that advanced stuff." There's nothing fancy about thinking and teaching "outside of the box." You'd be surprised at how a little fooling around with creative, progressive techniques can enhance a player's stick skills and self-confidence! Whether you're a mom who played lacrosse in college or a dad who has never picked up a stick, this chapter will familiarize you with how to teach progressive skills and techniques. We encourage all coaches of girls' lacrosse to purchase a *women's* lacrosse stick for your own use throughout the season. For the dads out there coaching girls' lacrosse, it's critical that you use a women's lacrosse stick when teaching and demonstrating skills. The sticks that girls play with don't have pockets as deep as boys' sticks, and you must understand the differences in how a girl's stick throws and catches in order to effectively teach the game. Go on! Have a catch with your new women's lacrosse stick! Develop your skills as your players develop theirs.

Basic Skills and How to Teach Them
Cradling

Cradling is the most important of the basic skills in girls' lacrosse. It involves keeping the ball in the pocket while the ball carrier is moving quickly (running) up the field or maneuvering through the defense. Mastering the cradling technique is much easier now that the cradle is a simpler, modified version of its former awkward self. Still, it may take some time to master. Having patience with your players as they are learning to cradle comfortably is extremely important and will go a long way in helping to build their confi-

Drills
- Cradle and Twirl F9
- Cradle and Extended Twirl F10
- Wall Ball Routine F11

dence. We want to stress teaching your players right away to practice cradling not only with their dominant hand up toward the top of the stick but also with their nondominant hand on top. This way they'll be comfortable sooner rather than later when various skills require them to switch hands.

For beginning players, here's a fun "homework assignment" to encourage use of both hands when playing lacrosse. Challenge your players to perform daily tasks—everything from brushing their teeth to using their fork—with their opposite hand. The rationale is that the more they use their "weak" hand in everyday life, the easier it will be to develop lacrosse skills with both hands. To further help dexterity in both hands, we'll introduce you to a number of stick-work tricks (see pages 109–15) that will produce confident and creative stick handlers and will encourage you and your players to have fun while learning to play lacrosse.

The grip. It's important to stress "soft hands" when gripping the stick. Beware of the death grip—squeezing so hard that the knuckles turn white. The bottom hand is the control hand and is placed at the bottom of the stick with the thumb wrapped around the stick and the cap on the end of the stick resting on the inside of the little finger. The top hand is the guide hand and does most of the work when cradling. The top hand grips the stick about a

Players should have soft hands while gripping the stick. Notice the bottom control hand's position. The top guide hand is placed one-third of the way down the stick. The stick rests in the palm but is controlled by the fingers.

third of the way down the shaft. The stick rests lightly in the palm of the top hand and is controlled by the fingertips.

Rocking motion. The motion of the fingers and wrist of the top hand curling together should be smooth and controlled. The top hand swings the stick from ear to nose, back and forth, using more wrist motion than elbow motion. Emphasize a smooth rocking motion so that the ball does not bounce around in the pocket. Ideally, the ball is cradled in the top half of the pocket by the shooting strings. Remind your players to relax their upper bodies and not to stiffen up their arms when cradling. A stiff, rigid cradle will lead to the ball popping out and lots of frustration! A smooth, fluid cradle will allow the ball to remain in the stick.

Tell your players to focus on the ear-to-nose cradle when handling the ball. The full cradle, or ear-to-ear cradle, should be reserved for dodging through defenders. The more subtle ear-to-nose cradle allows players to pass and shoot quickly and should be emphasized when working on cradling. Players should remember to give both hands equal time at the top of the stick.

Arm motion. The arms should be loose and relaxed. The top arm gives back and forth slightly with the rocking motion of the fingers and wrist of the top hand. The bottom arm holds the stick in front of the body and controls the base of the stick. The arms are relaxed and away from the body, not pulled in tight to the body.

Stick position. When first learning to cradle, the stick should be held at a slight angle on the side of the body by the ear (almost parallel with the body). The position of the stick will change based on the situation on the field and as a player's stick work develops. If there's no defensive pressure as a player is moving up the field, then the stick may be more horizontal to the ground while cradling and positioned at the player's hip. As the ball carrier approaches defensive pressure, the stick moves to a more vertical position— parallel with the body—to the side of the head for more protection. Even young lacrosse players will enjoy changing the level of their stick when they cradle; the more relaxed and comfortable they are, the better.

Two hands on the stick. It's important that players keep both hands on the stick while cradling. This allows for better control of the stick and the ability to pass or shoot quickly. Players could be called for a warding off foul if they take one hand off the stick and use their free arm to push off from another player while cradling through defenders. This results in loss of possession. When running in the open field, more advanced players can cradle one-handed with the stick extended out in front of them while pumping the other arm at their side, in a more natural running motion, to increase their speed.

Ground Balls

The ball spends an inordinate amount of time on the ground in girls' youth lacrosse. Picking up ground balls and gaining possession can make a tremendous difference in the success of your team. Ground balls are a terrific way to highlight the hustle of young players, so a strong and consistent emphasis should be placed on them in practices and in games. Three important points to emphasize whenever a player is going after a ground ball are to watch the ball all the way into the stick, keep moving, and, after gaining possession, try to move the ball immediately to a teammate.

Never allow your players to stand still and wait for a ground ball to roll to them. This is a bad habit to be nipped in the bud. Players should be able to pick up ground balls with either their dominant or nondominant hand on the bottom of the stick, so remember to have them switch hands while practicing pickups.

Stationary ground ball. At the youth level, especially when playing on grass, the ball often comes to a dead stop as soon as it hits the ground. Teaching your players how to pick up a stationary ground ball is a great introduction to picking up rolling ground balls. The two most important points to

Drills
- Ground Ball Tag **F20**
- Competitive Ground Balls **F21**
- Ground Ball Blob Passing **F22**

Top left: The way to approach a ground ball is to catch up and get low.

Top right: The stick is almost parallel to the ground and the knees are bent while the bottom hand pushes through the ground ball pickup.

Bottom left: While running through the ground ball pickup, the player immediately begins cradling.

Bottom right: The player explodes out of the ground ball pickup while protecting the stick.

emphasize when picking up stationary ground balls are to get alongside the ball and to bend at the knees to get low.

As a right-handed player approaches the ball, she puts her right foot slightly ahead of the ball, positions her head over the ball, and bends her knees to get low. She positions the stick head behind the ball and pushes through the pickup with her bottom hand; the top hand is the guide hand, but the bottom hand does most of the work. The stick is almost parallel to the ground as it moves through the pickup, and the bottom knuckles just about scrape the ground on the push-through. The player cradles the ball immediately and accelerates through the pickup.

Ground ball rolling toward. When a ground ball is rolling toward a player, she must continue running to the ball as quickly as possible. *Running through* a ground ball is an excellent habit. As the player approaches the ball, she extends her stick head to the ground on the side of her body (not out in front) so the angle of the stick is almost perpendicular to the ground. Her top hand should slide about a third of the way down the stick. Having the stick positioned almost perpendicular to the ground provides the maximum amount of surface space the stick has to offer for the ball to roll into. Picking the ball up on the side of her body allows the player to protect the ball from pesky defenders. As the ball enters the stick, the player must give backward with the stick toward her body so the ball doesn't pop out of her stick. She should bring the stick up to her head and begin cradling immediately. As with the cradle, players want to have soft hands when picking up ground balls that are rolling toward them. Giving with the momentum of the ball as it rolls into the stick and continuing to run through will ensure a smooth ground ball pickup.

Ground ball rolling away. The two most important points to emphasize to a player when picking up a ground ball that's rolling away are to catch up to the ball and to bend at the knees to get low.

Players too often reach out in front of themselves and bend at the waist (instead of at the knees) to try to pick up a rolling ground ball. As a result, they end up pushing the ball 40 yards down the field instead of picking it up!

First, the player catches up with the ball as quickly as possible. When she is alongside the ball, she bends at the knees and lowers her butt to the ground. Her dominant foot is in front of the ball, which guarantees that she's in proper position to pick it up. The player extends the stick head toward the ball, aiming just behind it. At the same time, the player's bottom hand also lowers so her stick is almost parallel to the ground. When the player is just about scraping her knuckles on the ground, she can effectively push through the pickup. The top hand guides the stick behind the ball, while the bottom hand pushes the stick through the ground ball pickup, just like shoveling snow. The player stays low until the ball is in her stick; standing up too soon can cause the ball to pop out of the pocket and can give an opponent an opportunity to play the ball. Once the ball is in the pocket, the player must begin cradling immediately, continue running through the pickup, and bring the stick up to her head to protect it from nearby defenders.

Picking up a ground ball under pressure. We just described picking up ground balls rolling to a player and away from a player, with no defensive pressure. What happens if there's another player battling for the same ground ball?

There are a few key points you want to teach your players when they are battling an opponent for a ground ball. As with an uncontested ground ball, the player must run to the ball as quickly as possible. She should be aware of the position of her opponent and get to the ball first, so she can step in front and block her opponent's path to the ball. Encourage her to use her back and legs to protect the ball while she's picking it up. It's important to stress running through the ground ball under pressure. Stopping the feet and batting at the ball are bad habits. If there are a number of other players around the ball, the player could consider flipping the ball away to a teammate who is waiting apart from the crowd. She must be careful not

A defender is ready to check as soon as the attacker has a ground ball in her possession.

to flip the ball up into an opponent but to flip it out and away from the crowd. This is a more advanced concept, best used with players who have an understanding of where their teammates are on the field.

The Pivot: Changing Direction

Learning to pivot instead of running in big semicircles to reposition themselves ("running around the barn") will enhance your players' ability to change direction quickly and help them to conserve energy. Running in semicircles allows defenders plenty of time and room to adjust their positions and continue marking the ball carrier.

When the ball carrier pivots to change direction, she plants either her left or right foot and turns on that foot as if it were nailed to the ground and explodes in the opposite direction. A quick change of direction and pushing off the pivot foot make the ball carrier much harder to defend and get the ball (and herself) moving quickly in the direction she wants to go. The ball carrier always wants to pivot away from the defense and keep her stick protected from the defense as she pivots.

How to pivot. Pivoting to the right requires the ball carrier to run forward and plant her left foot in front of the right foot with her weight evenly balanced. She then turns on the balls of her feet to the right until she faces the opposite direction. Her right foot is now in front, and she explodes out of the pivot by pushing off with her left foot and sprinting forward.

Pivoting to the left requires the ball carrier to run forward and plant her right foot in front of the left foot with her weight evenly balanced. She then turns on the balls of her feet toward her left until she faces the opposite direction. Her left foot is now in front, and she explodes out of the pivot by pushing off with her right foot and sprinting forward.

Lead with the stick. An important component of the pivot is protecting the stick from a defender while changing direction. When pivoting to the right, as the ball carrier plants her left foot she keeps her stick in the center of her body. As she turns, she gradually brings the stick in front of her, away from the defensive pressure, and leads with her stick as she explodes out of the pivot. A common mistake when pivoting is for ball carriers to plant their pivot foot, turn toward the opposite direction, and leave their stick exposed behind them for the defender to check. Leading with the stick will prevent the defender from checking on the change of direction.

Passing and Catching

The fastest game on two feet requires players to pass and catch accurately and consistently. When young players are first learning the game, the ball is on the ground a majority of the time. As the players become more proficient with their passing and catching, the game becomes more fluid and is extremely enjoyable to watch and coach. Once the fundamental techniques have been mastered, it's important to challenge your players to polish their stick work through repetition and creativity. You'll see your players' confidence soar as they become more accurate with their passes and more consistent with their catches. We suggest creative ways to develop your players' stick work on pages 109–15. When players are first learning how to pass and catch, they can remain stationary. However, as the players get more comfortable, a key point to emphasize during passing and catching drills is to keep moving. Encourage them to run through their passes and catches at every opportunity, just like they run through ground balls. This habit will improve their level of play tremendously.

Passing

Passing a lacrosse ball is similar to throwing a baseball. The same techniques are used to release the ball accurately. When throwing a baseball, a player rotates her hips and shoulders, reaches back with her throwing arm holding the ball above her head (not pushed from her chest), steps toward the target with her opposite foot, rotates her hips and shoulders toward the target and into the pass, snaps through the pass with her wrist, and follows through, completing the rotation of the hips and shoulders. The same technique applies when throwing a lacrosse ball.

Once beginning players become more comfortable with passing and catching, passing drills are done on the move. Make it a habit to keep your

Drills
- Partner Passing **F12**
- Triples **F13**
- Work-the-Point-Passing **F14**

Left: The first steps of an overarm pass. Notice that the player's arms are away from her body; she's reaching back while rotating her shoulder back, with the stick slightly above her head, as she steps in to her pass.

Right: As she releases the ball, the passer pushes with her top hand as she pulls with her bottom hand. The follow-through ends up across her body.

players moving while passing; movement will help with accuracy and momentum behind the ball.

Set the feet. The player begins by facing her passing partner. The passer's feet should be offset about shoulder-width apart. A right-handed player has her left foot in front of her right foot; a left-handed player has her right foot in front of her left foot.

Rotate the hips and shoulders. The passer rotates her hips and shoulders so that her shoulders are perpendicular to her passing partner and reaches back with her stick (similar to when throwing a ball). The top hand should be back and above the head (not in front of the body by the chest).

Hand and arm position. The passer's top hand slides about a third of the way down the stick. The thumb of the top hand is extended up the shaft of the stick, which helps the passer throw accurately. The bottom hand (positioned in front of the body) is at the bottom of the stick and provides the power for the pass. The passer's arms are relaxed and away from her body, not in tight by her sides.

The push-pull motion. The passer reaches back so that the head of her stick is behind her head and about 6 inches above her shoulder. The bottom hand must stay in front of the body and at chest height. If the bottom hand is raised higher than that, the stick will become parallel with the ground and the ball will either roll out of the pocket behind the passer or go straight up in the air on the release. The passer steps forward with her opposite foot (shifting her weight from the back foot to the front), drives the bottom arm forward, and then must execute a push-pull motion by using her top hand and arm to *push* the stick forward while the bottom hand and arm *pull* the stick toward the body. This motion makes the stick perform like a lever and produces direct, accurate passes. Encourage the passer to snap her wrist through the push motion as if she were throwing a ball. The follow-through of the stick should be across the body to the opposite hip—not under the armpit.

Completing the pass. As the passer steps into the pass and is completing the push-pull motion, her shoulders and hips are rotating through the pass, and her top arm should extend in the direction of the person she's passing to. The step forward, the rotation of the hips and shoulders, the snap of the wrist through the push-pull motion, and the follow-through of the stick across the body (to the opposite hip) give the pass its power. The accuracy of the pass is affected by the follow-through of the stick. If the follow-through is toward the ground, the pass will be low. If the follow-through is high, the pass will probably sail over her partner's head. Encourage your player to point with her stick (on her follow-through) exactly where she wants the pass to go, and her passes should be accurate.

The Flip Pass

The flip pass is a more advanced pass that releases from the player's hip and is used to pass around a defender's stick.

The same concepts apply to the flip pass as to a regular overhand pass. Out of the cradle, the passer drops her stick to waist level, parallel to the ground, with the ball resting near the throwing strings. The push-pull motion is used, with the bottom hand pulling toward the body while the top hand pushes from the hip. The player finishes the pass by snapping through with the wrist of the top hand and following through toward the target (as in the overhand pass).

Notice the parallel position of the stick during the flip pass.

The Behind-the-Back Pass

The behind-the-back pass is a more advanced technique to execute in game situations, yet it should be incorporated into practices because it's a lot of fun to do and helps even the newest player develop the ability to handle her stick.

Set the feet. The right-handed passer starts with her feet, hips, and shoulders perpendicular to the person she's passing to and with her right side facing away from the catcher.

Stick and arm position. The passer slides her top hand halfway down her stick and extends the stick back, behind, and even with her body, with her top arm outstretched (elbow slightly bent). The bottom hand is at the bottom of the stick and is positioned above the passer's right hip.

The push-pull motion. The passer steps with her left foot on a diagonal and leans slightly forward. She uses her bottom hand to push while her top hand pulls the stick toward the passer's right shoulder, where the pass is released. The stick shaft should make contact with the right shoulder, not the head! Make sure the passer is looking at her target as she executes the behind-the-back pass.

The Lob Pass

The lob pass is executed exactly as it sounds. The passer lobs the ball over the heads of the defenders to her teammate, who catches it over her shoulder on the run. It is an effective pass in starting an offensive fast break if the player receiving the ball can get a step on her defender. The lob pass can also be used to *switch the field* or send the ball from one side of the field to the other to move the ball into *open space*, away from defensive pressure.

Set the feet. Since the lob pass covers a lot of distance, the passer must shuffle into the pass to get momentum behind the rotation of her hips and shoulders. The passer's feet should be offset about shoulder-width apart. A right-handed player has her left foot in front of her right foot. A left-handed player has her right foot in front of her left foot. The passer shuffles forward a couple of steps while rotating her hips and shoulders back and reaching back with her stick. The passer can slide her top hand halfway down the shaft of the stick to get more leverage for the lob pass.

The release point. In order to make the lob pass "loopy" enough, the passer must release the ball while her stick is still slightly parallel to the ground on the throw. The follow-through ends up pointing toward the sky so the ball can get the height it needs.

Reverse-Stick Pass

The reverse-stick pass is an advanced technique that can be incorporated into practices through stick-work and wall ball drills (see chapter 10).

Set the feet. The player begins by facing her passing partner. A right-handed passer starts with her feet slightly offset, about shoulder-width apart, and with her right foot in front of the left.

Stick and arm position. The passer slides her top hand a third to halfway down her stick and cradles on her right side. She pulls the stick across her face from the right side of her head to the left, opening the head of the stick so it's facing her passing partner. To keep the ball in the pocket, she should hold the stick at a slight angle with the stick butt slightly out in front of her body; the bottom hand is farther out in front of the body than the top hand.

The push-pull motion. The passer steps with her right foot and uses her bottom hand to pull while her top hand pushes through the pass. It is important to keep the stick head at least 12 inches above the shoulders so the pass is direct and accurate.

Drills

- Wall Ball Routine `F11`
- Partner Passing `F12`
- Square Passing `F15`
- Triangle Passing `F18`

Catching

Catching the ball starts with watching the ball while it's in the air and following it into the pocket.

When working with younger players, have them exaggerate watching the ball into the pocket on the catch by instructing them to actually turn their head and look at the ball resting in the pocket as they catch it. Try hand-tossing balls to players (to minimize intimidation) and then comment on their ability to watch the ball into the pocket. As they become more proficient with their catches, they'll begin to see the ball peripherally instead of having to turn their heads. Throughout the season, challenge your players to catch at different levels, so they get used to handling a pass that may not be right at their stick. Always encourage your players to be moving toward the ball for the catch. For beginners, some passing and catching drills can be done while stationary. However, the sooner you get your players catching on the move, the more quickly their abilities will improve.

Set the feet. The player begins by facing her passing partner. The catcher's feet should be offset about shoulder-width apart. A right-handed player has her left foot slightly in front of her right foot. A left-handed player has her right foot slightly in front of her left foot.

Ask for the ball. As the catcher moves toward the passer, she asks for the ball by indicating her stick as a target to the passer. She holds her stick parallel to her body with her top hand placed slightly down the stick. The stick should be off to the side and slightly in front of her head when asking for the ball. The bottom hand is in front of the body, with the arm across the body at waist height. The head of the stick is slightly in front of the bottom hand to allow the player to give back with the ball on the catch. The catcher should never point her stick at the passer; she should keep her stick parallel to her body, in position to catch the ball, and she should immediately be able to cradle, pass, or shoot it.

Watch it in. As the ball comes toward the player who is catching, her eyes follow the ball at all times. Since women's lacrosse sticks don't have deep pockets, the player watches the ball into the pocket and gives back gently with the momentum of the ball as it enters the pocket, just as if she were catching an egg. As the ball approaches, the catcher doesn't move her stick toward the ball to meet it; instead, she's already giving back slightly as the ball enters the pocket so she actually catches it behind her ear in a position to protect the stick and begins cradling right away. Don't allow your players to bat at the ball. Encourage them to give with the ball as it enters the stick and to continue running through the catch.

Rotate the shoulders. As the catcher gives back with the ball, she rotates her shoulders slightly toward the side she's catching the ball on. The giving-back motion and the rotation of the shoulders help ease the ball into the pocket, protect the stick from defenders, and allow the player to cradle, pass, or shoot right away. As you are teaching your players to catch properly, continue to remind them to roll their shoulders on the catch and run through the catch.

Dodging

Dodging is a skill that every player on the field, no matter what her position, must understand and be able to execute. Whether an attacker's eluding a defender on the way to the cage, or a defender's trying to clear the ball past an attacker who's pressuring her, dodging effectively is vital. Before we get into specific dodging techniques, we want to emphasize that *speed* and *quickness* are a player's greatest assets. As a coach, you must recognize which players are fast and quick and must encourage them to use their speed to their advantage. A fancy dodge may not be necessary if a ball carrier can simply kick it into fifth gear and beat her opponent.

A player asks for the ball with her stick and watches the ball into her stick to complete a catch.

Drills

- Partner Dodging F23
- Pass and Dodge in Fours F24
- Five-on-Five Dodging Box F25
- Box Dodging F26

With that said, the purpose of a dodge is to *gain an advantage*. The most important aspect to remember when dodging is *not* to make preconceived moves; instead, learn to read the defense and adjust accordingly. There are several dodges in lacrosse. As your players develop, they will add their own variations to the basic dodging techniques. The main objective of a successful dodge is to get an opponent out of her defensive stance and off-balance. Players can use change of speed, change of direction, and quick movements of their head, shoulders, and stick to get their opponents out of their defensive stance and off-balance. Once an opponent is off-balance, the ball carrier can get a step on her and dodge to the opposite side. Before executing a dodge, the dodger often sets up her defender by faking a pass or shot. This is one way to get the defender out of her defensive stance. Here's how to do it.

The Face or Pull Dodge

The face or pull dodge is the easiest to teach and learn. It can be used in the midfield as well as in settled attack situations.

Set up the defender. As the dodger approaches her defender, she often sets up the defender by faking a pass or shot with a slight movement of her head and stick. This causes defenders to raise their stick and straighten up, taking them out of their defensive stance.

Stick position. The dodger keeps two hands on the stick, with the stick positioned parallel to the body and off the right shoulder (for a right-handed player). Once the dodger sets up the defender, she pulls the stick hard across her face to the opposite side, keeping the stick parallel to her body and protected from the defender. She may switch hands if she chooses, or keep the stick in her strong hand and bring it back to her strong side once past the defender.

Footwork. On the approach, the dodger jogs at the defender's left shoulder (as the defender is facing the dodger) to set her up with the fake pass or shot. When the dodger is within a stick's length of the defender, she plants her right foot (for a right-hander player), pulls her stick hard across her face, protecting the stick with her shoulders, and explodes past the de-

Left: The attacker looks to draw the defender out of the defensive stance by faking before a face dodge.

Center: The attacker pulls her stick across her body and protects it with her shoulder as she dodges past her defender.

Right: The attacker leads with her stick out of the face dodge with the defender trailing behind.

fender's right shoulder. As soon as the dodger gets a step ahead of the defender, she must cut the defender off by stepping back on the straight line with which she approached the defender, so the defender is left behind her. After an effective dodge, the defender will be looking at the dodger's back.

Lead with your stick. It's critical to lead with the stick out of every dodge. Once the dodger explodes past the defender, she should have her stick in front of her so her stick is protected at all times from the defender. The stick remains in front of the dodger until open space is gained, and she can pass or shoot as necessary.

The Dip Dodge

The dip dodge is similar to the change-of-hand dodge and sword dodge. The names of the dodges reflect technique, but they all have a common theme. The dodger switches her stick from one hand to the other to execute the move. Players must be able to cradle with both hands to execute these dodges.

Set up the defender. As the dodger approaches her defender, she sets up the defender by faking a pass or shot with a slight movement of her head and stick.

Stick position. The dodger keeps both hands on the stick as she approaches the defender, with the stick positioned parallel to the body and off the right shoulder (for a right-handed player). Once the dodger sets up the defender, she takes her left hand off the bottom of the stick and with her right hand dips the stick in front of her body (as if she were scooping the air in front of her body). She must turn her shoulders slightly to protect the stick as she brings it to her left side. Once the stick is on her left side, she grasps the top of the stick with her left hand, places her right hand on the bottom of the stick, and begins her cradle.

Footwork. On the approach, the dodger jogs at the defender's left

Left: The attacker dips her stick across her body to dodge a defender.

Center: The attacker switches hands and gets a step on her defender.

Right: The attacker leads with her stick out of the dip dodge, with the defender behind.

shoulder to set her up with the fake pass or shot. When the dodger is within a stick's length of the defender, she plants her right foot (for a right-handed player), dips her stick across the front of her body with her right hand while protecting the stick with her shoulders, switches the stick into her left hand, and explodes past the defender's right shoulder. As soon as the dodger gets a step ahead of the defender, she must cut off the defender so the defender is left behind her. Once the dodger explodes past the defender, she should hold her stick in front of her to protect it at all times from the defender.

Change-of-Hands Dodge

The change-of-hands dodge is executed like the dip dodge, but instead of dipping the stick across the front of the body to change hands the dodger pulls the stick from one side of her body, across her face, to the other side of her body and then switches hands. For example, a right-handed dodger pulls the stick across her face from her right side to her left side. As the stick is moving from one side of the body to the other, the dodger slides her left hand up to the top of the stick and then grasps the bottom of the stick with her right hand, completing the switch. She begins her cradle right away with the stick in her left hand.

Sword Dodge

The sword dodge is executed like the dip dodge and the change-of-hands dodge. Instead of dipping the stick across the front of the body or pulling it across the face to change hands, the right-handed dodger slides the stick down to her left hand, which is at her waist, in a motion that is like sliding a sword into its sheath. Then she brings the stick up in her left hand to her left side while the right hand grasps the bottom of the stick. This is executed in two smooth motions: the slide down from the right side and the slide back up to the left side. The footwork and the method of protecting the stick with the shoulders is the same for all three dodges.

Roll Dodge

The roll dodge is used primarily in settled situations to gain space directly behind a defender. The player can perform a roll dodge to the left or right, depending on her position on the field and whether she is right- or left-handed.

Set up the defender. As with all dodges, the dodger often sets up the defender by faking a pass or shot with a slight movement of her head, shoulders, and stick.

Stick position. The dodger keeps two hands on the stick as she approaches the defender and holds her stick positioned parallel to the body and off the right shoulder (for a right-handed player).

Footwork. On the approach for a right-handed dodger, the dodger jogs at the defender's left shoulder to set her up with a fake pass or shot. When the dodger is within a stick's length of the defender, the dodger plants her left foot (for a right-handed player) in front of and between the defender's feet. The left foot serves as the pivot foot for the roll dodge while the right foot serves as the swing foot. Once the left foot is planted between the defender's feet, the dodger rolls to her right, swinging her right foot around the defender. As the dodger rolls to her right, her back is toward the defender,

Top left: An attacker sets up a defender in an attempt to get her out of the defensive stance before executing a roll dodge.

Top right: The attacker (right) plants her left foot and rolls to the right while protecting her stick.

Bottom left: The attacker completes her roll, keeping the defender behind her, and leads with her stick.

Bottom right: The attacker explodes out of the roll dodge, leading with her stick and looking at the goal cage.

and she must keep her stick between her shoulders through the roll to protect it. The right foot will now be to the side and slightly behind the defender as the roll is complete, and the dodger explodes forward with her left foot while cutting the defender off with her body. Once the dodger explodes past the defender, she should have her stick in front of her so that it is protected at all times from the defender.

Drills

- Triple Shot F27
- Star Shooting F28
- Shooting Shuttle F29
- Lead with Your Head
  F30

Shooting

Shooting is so much more than simply throwing the ball at the cage. It's a skill that takes lots of practice to master. Encourage all your players to shoot, no matter what their positions are on the field. Everyone likes to score goals, and the defenders will have just as much fun doing shooting drills as the attackers. When teaching your players how to shoot, build on the passing skills they've already learned. The overhand shooting motion is similar to the passing motion, and as your players become more comfortable, you can introduce the more advanced shooting techniques. The types of shots the attackers use will depend on where they are on the field, where the defense is positioned, and where the goalie is positioned. Shooters should develop a variety of shots. The three most important components of shooting are *power*, *placement*, and *creativity*. Shooting drills must be set up to develop all three components and should be done at every practice.

Release points. Shooters can release the ball from a variety of release points—overhand, three-quarter arm, side arm, and risers, which rise from low to high. The most accurate release point is the overhand shot. This should be taught first and practiced consistently.

Down the pipes. You always want to encourage shooters to go "down the pipes." This refers to the pipes of the goal cage, and involves teaching your players to get to the center of the goal cage between the goal pipes to get the best angle to shoot. Shooting from the center of the goal cage gives the attacker the best opportunity to score because she has the most areas of the cage to choose from.

The Overhand Shot

The stance. The shooter begins by facing the goal with her feet offset and shoulder-width apart. A right-handed shooter has her left foot in front, and a left-handed shooter has her right foot in front.

Hips, arms, hands, and feet. The shooter rotates her hips so her shoulders are perpendicular to the goal as she reaches back with her stick. Her arms are away from her body, not in tight by her side. Her top hand slides about one-third of the way down the stick while the bottom hand is at the bottom of the stick. The thumb of the top hand is extended up the shaft of the stick, which will help with the accuracy of the shot. As the shooter pulls the stick back, her top hand should be about 6 inches higher than the shoulder and her bottom hand should be slightly below the shoulder. As she rotates her hips and reaches back with her stick, she transfers her weight to her back foot. When she begins the shooting motion she shifts her weight from her back foot to her front foot and steps toward the goal with her front foot. Her stick is positioned behind her head, which will make the goalie lose sight of the ball for a second.

The shooting motion. The shooter first drives her bottom hand forward while stepping toward the goal and rotating her hips toward the goal. She then pushes her top hand forward toward the cage while pulling the bottom hand back toward her body. The *pushing* of the top hand and the *pulling* of the bottom hand act as a lever and, combined with the rotation of the hips and shoulders, provide the power for the shot.

The follow-through. The shooter completes the shooting motion by following through across her body as her hips, shoulders, and back foot com-

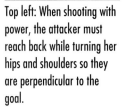

Top left: When shooting with power, the attacker must reach back while turning her hips and shoulders so they are perpendicular to the goal.

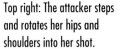

Top right: The attacker steps and rotates her hips and shoulders into her shot.

Bottom left: The attacker follows through with a snap of her wrist and completes the rotation of her hips and shoulders.

Bottom right: The attacker's back foot follows through, completing the motion that goes into a power-packed overhand shot.

plete their rotation. The top arm should extend fully toward the spot the shooter was aiming for, which helps with the accuracy of the shot. The overhand shooting motion is very similar to the passing motion and can result in a high shot or a low shot, depending on the follow-through.

Bounce Shots

A follow-through toward the ground results in a hard bounce shot. Any goalie will tell you that low, hard bounce shots are tough to save. The shooter can bounce the ball at the top of the crease, attempting to have the ball bounce over the goalie's shoulder as she drops down to save it, or the shooter can bounce the ball right behind the goalie's feet toward either corner of the cage for another high-percentage shot. Here's a more advanced technique that's fun to practice: Try putting a spin on bounce shots. Teach your players to spin the ball as it comes out of their stick by using a tennis analogy. To put a side spin on a bounce shot, the shooter twists the stick over the top of the ball on the release and follow-through, causing the ball to skip to the left when it hits the ground. To execute a side spin to the right with a lacrosse stick, the shooter rolls the stick underneath the ball at the last second in her release so the ball will skip to the right as it hits the ground. A spin on bounce shots will make them even harder for the goalie to save.

Additional Release Points

As we mentioned earlier, the three components of shooting are power, placement, and creativity. Additional release points that increase power include a three-quarter arm shot, a side arm shot, and riser shots. All these release points use the same push-pull concept. Have your players practice shooting from every level so they become comfortable with each one.

Placement

You'll often see a shooter execute a terrific dodge, find herself in front of the goal, shoot, and miss the cage completely. Or the player shoots the ball directly into the goalie's stick and wastes a golden opportunity to score. This happens at every level of the game because the shooter fails to do one thing—look before she shoots! Placement of shots is critical to scoring. Get your players in the habit of leading with their head before they shoot.

Lead with your head. As the shooter draws her stick back to begin the shooting motion, and before she steps into her shot, she must lead with her head by looking at the cage to find the open net. She is looking to see the location of defenders, the position of the goalie, and the open areas of the goal to shoot for. Leading with the head combined with following through greatly increases the accuracy of a player's shots. When teaching shooting, ask your players, "What do you see when you look at the goal?" If they answer, "The goalie," stress to them that they need to see the *net* behind the goalie: that's what they are shooting at!

Creativity

The final component of successful shooting is creativity. Offensive players should practice taking shots from many different locations on the field: low-angle shots, outside shots, high shots, bounce shots, shots right on top of the crease, and so on. Behind-the-back shots, around-the-world shots, extended-stick shots, between-the-legs shots are all creative ways to surprise a goalie and score. They also make for fun shooting practices!

Left: An attacker sets up for a behind-the-back shot. Notice her top hand has slid down the stick.

Right: An attacker releases a behind-the-back shot over her shoulder. Notice her looking at the cage.

Fakes are another way to be creative while shooting. Using a head-and-shoulders fake high and then shooting low is very effective. The objective in using a fake is to get the goalie moving so you can shoot around her. Dipping the shoulder and stick low and shooting high will catch a goalie by surprise. These are all methods offensive players can use to shoot creatively (yes, even the 6-year-olds). Have fun with your shooting drills. Allow your girls to be creative, and watch their confidence soar along with their shooting ability.

Quick-Stick Shot

A quick-stick shot is exactly like it sounds: the shooter receives the feed and quickly redirects it toward the cage. To do so, the shooter gives back with the ball on the catch and immediately snaps through the shot using the push-pull motion (without cradling) to redirect it to the cage. This is an advanced shot that takes lots of practice to master. The *feeder,* the player who passes the ball to a player who catches it and shoots on goal, generally sends a high pass to the shooter, who is able to watch the ball into her stick, give back slightly to gain control of the ball, and then immediately redirect the ball as a shot on the cage with a snap of her wrists.

Direct Free-Position Shot

A direct free-position shot in women's lacrosse is similar to a foul shot in basketball. A direct free-position shot is awarded to an offensive player when a defender commits a major foul (3 seconds, shooting space, etc.) inside the 8-meter arc. The offensive player is placed 8 meters from the goal on one of seven hash marks that are evenly placed around the 8-meter arc. The player shoots from the hash mark closest to where the foul occurred. Any players inside the arc must clear out of the arc at the closest point and must be at least 4 meters from the fouled player. The player who committed the foul is positioned on the 12-meter fan directly behind the player with the ball. Players must stand on the whistle, or stop when the whistle blows, so those already outside the arc remain where they are as long as it is 4 meters from the fouled player. On the official's whistle to restart play, the offensive player tries to score while the defensive players try to gain good defensive position to prevent or block the shot.

Back up the cage. The offense should have a player behind the cage on an 8-meter shot to back up the shot. A missed shot may present another opportunity to score so long as the team can maintain possession. If an offensive player is not already behind the cage on an 8-meter shot, communicate to your players who will back up the cage so they are prepared to run after the ball once the shot is taken.

An attacker shoots with power by stepping into her shot, rotating her hips and shoulders, and following through.

Ready position. When the offensive player is positioned on the hash mark, she assumes a ready position so that she's prepared to shoot as soon as the whistle blows. It's a matter of personal preference which foot the offensive player leads with; we recommend encouraging your players to try taking free-position shots starting with the left foot in front on the hash as well as with the right foot in front. Whichever foot is on the hash, the opposite foot is back for balance, the knees are bent, and the offensive player leans slightly forward on the balls of her feet. She is ready to explode toward the cage on the whistle. The stick position is also a matter of personal preference. The offensive player can set up with her stick in front of her, she can turn her shoulders to the side and place her stick behind her head, she can start with the stick in one hand, and so on. Be creative!

The Outside Shot

One way to shoot from the 8-meter arc is to take an outside shot from the hash mark as soon as the official blows her whistle. This allows the offensive player to release the shot quickly and avoid as much defensive pressure as possible. Younger players may not be as strong physically; they may not get the ball to the cage with much power. However, a well-placed outside bounce shot could catch a goalie by surprise. Have your offensive player in her ready position on the 8-meter arc, with her shoulders turned to the sideline and her stick back to shoot. On the whistle, she takes a shuffle step inside the 8-meter arc at an angle away from the defender on her stick side. This gives the offensive player a bit more time to get the shot off and avoid the defender on her stick side. She then rotates her hips, shoulders, and arms on her outside shot and snaps through the shot with her wrist. We generally recommend a low shot or a bounce shot for our younger players but encourage the older players to try some riser shots. Once the shot is away, your players inside the 8-meter arc should be ready for a rebound from the goal, and your players outside the arc should be ready for a save and *goalie clear* (a pass from the goalie to a defender who looks to move the ball out of the defensive end).

Take it in. Another offensive option on the 8-meter shot is to take the ball into the 8-meter arc at an angle to get off a higher-percentage shot closer to the cage. The key is to burst into the 8-meter arc at enough of an angle to cut off one defender while drifting away from the defender on the stick side.

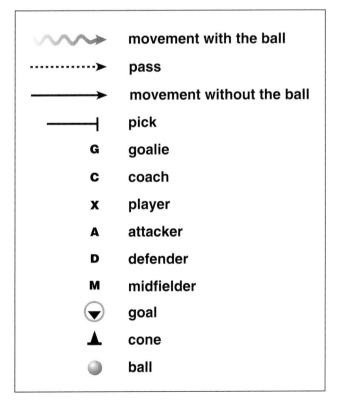

∿∿∿⟶	**movement with the ball**
┈┈┈┈┈▷	**pass**
⟶	**movement without the ball**
⊢	**pick**
G	**goalie**
C	**coach**
X	**player**
A	**attacker**
D	**defender**
M	**midfielder**
▼	**goal**
▲	**cone**
●	**ball**

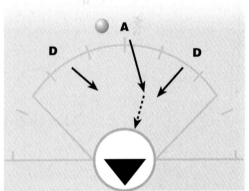

Above: Take it in. A right-handed player taking an 8-meter shot should veer away from the defender on her strong side so she can take a quality shot.

Left: Diagram key.

Feeding

Feeding is the ability to pass the ball accurately to a teammate, giving her a quality opportunity to score. Constant movement, seeing the field, timing the feed, and stick protection are the four elements of successful feeding.

Feeding from behind the crease. A unique component of girls' lacrosse is that players are allowed to use the space behind the crease, or goal circle, to feed the ball. Once in a settled offensive situation, teams move the ball to X, or point behind, the area directly behind the goal cage, to allow their offense to set up and to force the defense to reposition in order to find the ball. This is a terrific spot to feed from, as it's very difficult for defenders to play the ball behind the goal without running the risk of the ball carrier dodging to the cage from behind and using the crease to gain an advantage on her defender.

Constant movement. Players must be able to feed with and without defensive pressure. In order to do so, feeders must constantly be moving to make it difficult for defenders to play them. This reduces the possibility of their feeds being blocked or intercepted by defenders. Teach your players to drive toward their defenders and then take a few steps away from them to create the space needed to feed and to get the defenders out of their defensive stance. Encourage your players to *curl* upfield when passing from behind the goal to increase their passing lane and get a better angle for feeding their teammate. Feeders must be able to pass off their back foot (with their weight on the back foot) accurately while they are avoiding defenders (this is a more advanced concept).

Seeing the field. Feeders must be aware of where their teammates are on the field and must anticipate cutters. To do so, feeders must keep their head up and constantly scan the field to read where the next cutter is coming from. *Cutters* are attackers who accelerate to create space and passing opportunities.

Timing the feed. Good timing is the key to feeding. Again, the feeder is responsible for giving the player receiving the ball a quality opportunity to score. If the feed comes too early, the cutter may not be ready for it. If the feed comes too late, the cutter may no longer be at a good angle to score, or the defense may have already recovered.

Stick protection. Using fakes, changing the level of the stick on the feed, and protecting the stick while assessing cutters are important factors for the feeder to consider. Feeders must remember to turn their shoulders for protection and hold their stick way back behind their head.

Stick Checking

Stick checking at the youth level is a topic of hot debate for many people involved in women's lacrosse. US Lacrosse wants to send a consistent message regarding checking to youth players: Players below the seventh-grade level should not be stick checking. The US Lacrosse Rules Committee hopes that the no-checking mandate will allow beginning players to work on the basic fundamentals of the game—passing, catching, footwork, proper positioning, and marking—before they're introduced to the more advanced skill of stick checking. Players on interscholastic seventh- and eighth-grade teams are allowed to use modified checking (checking the stick below shoulder level) as an intermediate step toward full checking. Recreation league teams of players ages 10 and up may also use the modified checking rule. US Lacrosse hopes that modified checking will allow older youth players to learn proper checking skills, while at the same time encouraging good cradling and stick-handling skills for the attack player.

We believe that girls' lacrosse players should be taught the correct way to check as soon as they are physically and mentally able to control their actions and make conscientious decisions; there's no one set age. It's a skill that must be practiced and developed over a period of time. As important as the actual technique of correctly checking is the ability to maintain self-control when checking. This occurs over many practices and games and is something that players, coaches, and officials have a hand in controlling.

With that said, here's the correct way to teach stick checking. Stick checking is the striking on the corner of an opponent's stick by a defender who is trying to dislodge the ball from the stick. Stick checks should be controlled, short, quick taps. The defender's stick makes contact with the outside top corner of the ball carrier's stick, turning the stick so the ball falls out. There's no backswing when checking, and there should be no sweeping follow-through. Use the phrase "check and release" when describing and practicing stick checking with your players. The defender must establish good body position before checking. She must be alongside of or slightly in front of the ball carrier before she checks. A defender may never check toward the head or body. A defender may also check from behind (trail check) as long

Left: A defender executes a picture-perfect check below the waist on the attacker's stick.

Right: Checking the corner of the stick and releasing quickly should effectively dislodge a ball from an attacker's stick.

as she doesn't reach across the attacker's body from behind and try to check. A defender must always check away from the head or body. Maintaining body position is of the utmost importance. We teach our players not to check unless they are 90 percent sure they can come up with the ball. Many players throw stick checks and then become off-balance and out of position. As a rule of thumb, teach your players to concentrate on good body position and be judicious about the number of checks they attempt and how and when they attempt them.

The 3-Second Count

All youth levels (A, B, and C) are subject to a 3-second count, which is designed to reward good defense where the no-checking rule is in force. An offensive player may not hold the ball for more than 3 seconds when she is closely guarded, or marked, by a defender, and the defender is in a position to legally check (if checking were allowed). Once the defender is in good defensive position with an opportunity to check (if it were allowed), the umpire gives an audible 3-second count. The attacker, upon hearing the 3-second count, must reposition her stick away from the defender or pass the ball, making a legal check impossible. Otherwise, she loses possession. The defender must have two hands on her stick during the 3-second count.

The defender (right) slides her hands down her stick so she can reach high enough to block a pass by the attacker.

Blocking and Intercepting

Blocking and intercepting are two defensive skills that are rarely practiced but are invaluable on the field. They both require anticipation, good timing, and hand-eye coordination on the defender's part. With practice, these skills can be developed and can make a big difference in gaining possession of the ball.

Blocking. The defender must be positioned to the side of the ball carrier when blocking a pass or shot so she doesn't get hit with the ball or the follow-through. She tries to mirror the ball carrier's stick with her own, and as the ball carrier releases the pass or shot, the defender extends her stick vertically by sliding the stick through the top hand to meet the ball as it leaves the stick, blocking the pass or shot. The timing of the stick extension is critical and coincides with anticipating the ball carrier's pass. Once the ball is blocked, the defender must step in front of her opponent, between the opponent and the ball, and pick up the ground ball.

Intercepting. Intercepting a pass is one of the most exciting skills a player can execute. It means a surprise change of possession. Interceptions happen when a player reads or anticipates where the other team is going to pass the ball. She then steps in front of the intended receiver and catches the pass, gaining possession from the opponent. When intercepting a pass, the top hand slides about two-thirds of the way down the stick shaft to give the player as much reach as possible while still being able to control the stick. The player must make a quick burst into the passing lane while stepping in front of the intended receiver. Once the interception is made, the player with the ball brings her stick in front of her and cuts off her opponent so she won't get checked from behind. As always, the player accelerates through the catch.

Center Draw Techniques

Drill
• Center Draw 08

There are two components of the center draw. First, the player taking the draw tries to control the direction of the ball and second, her teammates around the center circle try to gain possession of the ball once it's put into play. There are a number of techniques that can be used to win the center draw. A key factor is the player first getting the ball on the back of the pocket of her stick in order to control the ball. Quick wrist movement on the whistle is critical in gaining control of the ball. Once the player taking the draw is in control of the ball, she can try to do a number of things.

- direct the ball straight up and take possession of it herself (while her teammates box out their opponents on the circle)
- send the ball long for a teammate
- send the ball short inside the circle; her teammates can try to box out their opponents and come up with possession

Players positioned on the outside of the circle need to communicate with each other to determine who will take the *short draw* (inside the circle) and who will go for the *long draw* that typically sails over the heads of the players on the circle.

In order to win the center draw and direct the ball where she wants it to go, the player taking the draw must be aware of some key points when executing the draw.

- The player who is quickest to get under the ball by rotating her wrist on hearing the whistle will most likely be in control of the direction of the ball.
- In order to get under the ball the player must position her top hand as close to the head of the stick as possible to give her the power to dig the ball out of her opponent's stick with the corner of her stick.
- The player should experiment with her stance when taking the center draw. A tremendous amount of power comes from the rotation of the player's legs, hips, shoulders, and arms. Players should practice having both feet parallel to the center line or the left foot toeing the line with the right foot set back.
- If the back of the player's stick is facing her goal, and her back is facing

her goal, she is using more of a pulling motion to get under the ball. We recommend that the player have her right foot toeing the line and her left foot at an angle behind her so the natural rotation of her hips and shoulders allow her to comfortably get under the ball and propel it up and away.

- If the player and the back of her stick are facing her goal, she is using more of a pushing motion to get under the ball. This requires more arm and upper body strength, yet it can be very effective when directing the ball specifically to a teammate positioned on the center circle.

The center draw must be practiced over and over again. Have your center draw players (it's always good to have at least two designated players who can take the draw) practice the draw techniques as their warm-up or when their teammates are doing stick-work tricks. All they need is a line and a bucket of balls—it's not always necessary to have a coach set up each draw.

CHAPTER 6

The Fundamentals of Offense

The team in possession of the ball has one main objective: to score! Maintaining possession of the ball will prevent the other team from scoring. The offensive team uses its passing, dodging, and shooting abilities to beat the defense and create quality scoring opportunities. Offensive success comes from having players who can

- execute fundamental skills consistently
- make quality decisions with and without the ball
- communicate well with each other
- understand their roles in relation to the ball

In this chapter, we introduce team offensive concepts and some basic offensive formations that will help your players create quality scoring opportunities.

> Hot spots are designated areas on the field used during settled offensive play.

Designated Hot Spots

When you're first teaching settled-attack concepts, it's helpful to designate *hot spots*, areas on the field from which you want your team to attack. We've found that giving numbers to these areas around the goal makes it much easier to explain positions on the field. See the diagram for how to number the offensive end of the field.

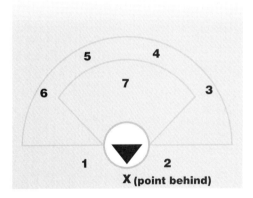

Position one offensive player in each of these hot spots around the goal to balance the field. The seventh offensive player has the option of playing on the inside of the 8-meter arc or taking the top center position to balance the attack outside the 8-meter arc. X (point behind) designates the area directly behind the center of the goal.

With the use of designated numbered areas on the field, your players will clearly understand where you want them to dodge from, pick to, clear out of, move toward, and so on. For example, "Jane, clear out of the 4-spot because we want Sarah to dodge from the 3-spot." Or, "Girls, we need to balance the field. Let's get everyone to a hot spot so we're not so congested around the ball."

The Restraining Line

The restraining line limits the number of offensive and defensive players in front of the goal at any given time. In youth lacrosse, the restraining line allows seven offensive players and seven defensive players plus the goalie to be inside the 30-yard line on each end of the field. Any seven attackers and any seven defenders can go over the restraining line to play in a settled situation. It's important in transitioning the ball from one end of the field to the other to communicate who is going over and who is staying back so there isn't an offside foul. However, offensively, many teams designate four attackers and three midfielders who can go over. Subsequently, there are four designated defenders along with the three midfielders. The midfielders are responsible for playing both offense and defense and are usually the fastest and most fit players on the team. We encourage you to develop *complete* players in your practices who'll feel comfortable inside the restraining line either on offense or on defense. For example, if one of your attackers beats one of your defenders down the field and finds herself on defense inside the restraining line, she'll have no problem fitting into the defensive unit if you've put her in that situation at practice. Your attackers should know how to play defense, and your defenders should know how to play offense; this strategy will pay off in the players' development as complete players throughout their lacrosse career.

The Fast Break

Because it's played in the air, girls' lacrosse is fast-paced. Players often find themselves in fast-break situations, which offensively can put you a player up on your opponents and defensively can find you a player down. It's important to work with your team so they'll recognize a player-up advantage and make the most of it. When transitioning the ball from the defensive end of the field to the offensive end, the attacking team may get a step ahead of their opponents, creating a six-on-five, a five-on-four, a four-on-three, and so on. Essentially, any situation where the offensive team outnumbers the defensive team is a fast break. **02 03 04**

The Ball Carrier

The player with the ball must recognize, as well as anticipate, what's happening off the ball and react accordingly. She must first recognize if there's a fast-break opportunity as she's bringing the ball upfield. Once the ball is settled,

The Complete Player

Why settle for churning out one-dimensional players when you can just as easily develop players who are comfortable on both sides of the field? To do this, make sure your drills run continuously—meaning when the defense gets the ball, it transitions to offense, and vice versa.

Try setting up a short field. Bring the goals in close to make a 40-yard field for a three-on-three. The offensive team gives it their best shot. When the ball turns over, the defense becomes offense. This way attackers develop defensive skills and defensive players learn attacking skills. Attackers will be better equipped to beat defenders (and vice versa) if they understand defensive concepts and can play defense.

During these offensive and defensive combinations, coaches need to stop play occasionally to discuss possession as well as throwing and catching skills; don't allow players to simply run the ball. Also discuss on- and off-ball defensive positioning. You and your assistant coach can have two short games going at one time. One coach can focus on offensive concepts such as spacing, throwing and catching, and cutting. The other can concentrate on defensive positioning, double-teaming, and clearing. Then switch. This way, your players will get a variety of input.

We can't emphasize enough the benefits to offensive players of understanding the defensive role: to see and feel the game from both perspectives. At the youth level, everybody should have the opportunity to play at various positions. Everyone needs to play a certain amount in each game. Versatility with positioning and giving every player time to develop in real game play benefits the entire team.

This switching of attack and defense might cost your team the finely tuned synergy that can develop among a core group of offensive or defensive players who practice together as a unit and therefore know each other's abilities and idiosyncrasies. But the benefit is that they're all developing into complete players who will have a comprehensive understanding of the game. Another benefit is that you're allowing players to evolve into positions of choice, based on the fact that they've had an opportunity to experience all positions and all facets of the game. The youth level is the time and place for girls to experiment; it's hardly the time and place to pigeonhole someone.

Society tells us that everyone wants to win. And society will question a coach for playing kids in positions at which they're not as strong as others might be. But try to think of winning in terms of giving as many kids as possible as many opportunities as possible to discover their strengths and challenge their weaknesses. Try to think that all kids win when they improve their skills, develop game sense, and recognize the importance of working together as a team. When Suzy Jane is playing center, and she isn't as strong as Sarah might be, then the team concept tells us that her teammates need to pick up any slack. This spirit of cooperation will benefit everyone.

Perhaps the most important benefit of all is that if kids are allowed to play, they might just stick with lacrosse instead of dropping out. Keep in mind that you're bearing witness to an early stage of budding athletes. To discourage enthusiasm for sport at this age is a much greater loss than any trouncing on the field. Some kids will develop later than others; don't ruin their chances to enjoy sport. Don't ruin a love they don't yet have. Your purpose is to build lacrosse players, not destroy athletic ambition.

As the players get older, they'll ultimately choose or fall into their preferred positions. This will happen naturally if you've introduced them to the whole game in a way that encouraged them to stick with the sport and go on.

We can't change those coaches or parents whose sole goal is winning a game. But we'd like to. At the recreational level, there are certain crucial philosophies that need to govern a coach's decision making. Parents may require your guidance in their expectations of you and your team. With young athletes, the focus needs to be on teaching skills as well as nurturing a love of sport and competition through unabashed play. It's OK to be organized, intense, and competitive, but above all, keep it fun. The best thing you can do for your players is to help them develop a love for lacrosse, and sport in general. Identify your philosophy as a coach and stick with it.

she must be able to dodge, draw a double team, feed, and shoot. The ball carrier should check the cage whenever there's an opportunity and challenge her defender in a one-on-one situation. As she challenges, she must be aware of what her teammates are doing off the ball and what the defense is doing. If she draws a double team (has two defenders on her), the ball carrier will look to back out of double-team pressure (drawing the defense with her) and pass the ball to an open teammate. If the defense doesn't slide and double-team her, she takes the one-on-one to the cage and looks to shoot the ball around the goalie.

Off-Ball Players

Only one person at a time can have the ball, so the other six offensive players must be moving to do one of three things: create space for the ball carrier, be an outlet for the ball carrier, or occupy a defender. Being an outlet for the ball carrier means providing an option for her to pass to if she needs it. Occupying a defender means that the player moves in such a way that her defender pays attention to her and not the person with the ball. We also call this playing a defender. Teach offensive players without the ball to play their defenders in one of the following ways.

Create space. If a player is adjacent to the ball carrier and the ball carrier has a good opportunity to dodge, the adjacent player must play her defender by cutting hard at the defender and taking her away from the ball carrier. This creates space for her teammate to dodge and forces the defender to pay attention to the cutter and not the dodger.

Be an outlet. The player with the ball needs someone to pass to if she's being pressured or doesn't have a good opportunity to dodge to the goal. An off-ball player can give her an outlet, or a passing option, by executing a V-cut, in which the offensive player cuts in toward her defender and then cuts hard away from her defender and toward the ball (moving in the shape of a V) to gain the needed space to receive the ball without defensive pressure.

Set a pick. Picks are used in many sports to create offensive opportunities. Setting a pick requires one player to come to a legal position while her teammate directs her defender toward the pick, allowing the player setting the pick to block the path of the defender (forcing her to stop or change direction) and the attacker to gain an advantage into open space. In the game of lacrosse a pick can be set on and off the ball to free teammates for shots on goal or to produce uneven situations in the offense's favor. It's important to set a proper pick that consists of a legal position and an element of surprise. The player setting the pick is trying to get the defender to take a couple of extra steps to get around her, subsequently allowing her offensive teammate to get ahead of the defender being picked. When setting a pick for a teammate who has the ball, the picker must be prepared to accept contact and, after the pick is set, *flash* to the ball, or move as quickly as possible to open space. This will negate the defensive strategy of switching. The player who is getting picked for must be ready to draw a double team and move away from the defensive pressure in order to pass the ball to her open teammate.

When setting a pick, it's important to keep the stick straight up and down, not parallel with the ground. Having the stick parallel to the ground when setting the pick could result in it holding the defender, which is a foul. It's also a foul to set a *blind pick* (a pick which the defender doesn't have time to react to). To avoid setting a blind pick the pick should be set off to one side or the other of a defender. Remaining stationary until a teammate runs off the pick is not mandatory; the player can move as long as the defender has time and space to react.

Cut off a pick. Players on the off-ball side should expect their teammates to set a pick for them and should look to cut off the pick, asking for the ball. It's the job of the person the pick is being set for to use the pick effectively. She must play her defender first by making a move away from where she wants to go (to get the defender to turn toward her), and then as the pick is set, she must cut back into the pick and run off the shoulder of the player who sets the pick. **F31**

Make backdoor cuts. If a defender is ball watching, the attacker should simply make a backdoor cut behind her to the goal and look for a feed. Teach the offensive player to move into a space that will force her defender to turn her head to find the ball. Once the defender turns her head for that split second, the offensive player bursts behind her, asking for the ball.

Since so many girls' lacrosse players wear their hair in ponytails, we teach our players to "cut to the ponytail" on a backdoor cut; this reminds them to cut behind their defender when she turns her head to find the ball.

Switch positions. Teach your players that they should never stand completely still on offense. Standing still makes playing defense easy for the other team and doesn't benefit fellow offensive players. An off-ball attacker should switch positions with the player adjacent to her by playing the defender first (by cutting at or behind the defender for a couple of steps to make the defender pay attention to the attacker) and then should switch positions with the player next to her, who has done the same thing. Playing the defender and then switching with an adjacent teammate forces the defense to pay attention to the off-ball attacker and may give the ball carrier the time she needs to get to the goal without added defensive pressure.

Balance the field. Off-ball attackers are also responsible for balancing the field. As they're moving to create space and scoring opportunities for the ball carrier, they must be aware of where they are on the field and must keep proper balance on settled attack. If the attackers are all bunched together, it's easy for the defense to guard them. If they're too close to the ball, the ball carrier has nowhere to go and has lots of defenders ready to play her.

Keep the stick perpendicular to the ground when setting a pick. *Maryalice Yakutchik*

Balancing the field and timing cuts to the ball (both have to be done simultaneously) are the most difficult concepts for young lacrosse players to understand and execute. This is where having designated hot spots on the field can help your players balance the field on your command. The next section will help you teach your players how to keep the field balanced through offensive formations.

Settled Offensive Sets

Once the offense has transitioned the ball and there's no fast-break opportunity, they must try to score in a settled offensive situation, or *set*. In a settled offense, the attack unit maintains possession, passes the ball around the 8-meter arc, and cuts, sets picks, and creates space in an attempt to create quality scoring opportunities. For beginning players, the focus should be on maintaining space for the ball carrier—not all cutting to the ball at once—and creating one-on-one situations where they'll challenge defenders to the cage. Very often you'll see a group of 6- to 8-year-old players get the ball down on offense, but they'll take so long making a move to the cage that they end up losing possession. Encourage quick transition to the offensive end of the field. Encourage your attackers to make the appropriate number of passes before they can shoot (often three passes are required), and send them to the cage!

There are a number of sets or formations you can utilize for your attack, depending on what your attackers' strengths are as a unit and what the defenders' weaknesses are. The following offensive sets are described from the top center of the 12-meter fan to X (point behind). Within each set, the ball carrier is looking to check the cage, dodge, draw a double team, feed, or shoot. The off-ball attackers are looking to create space for the ball carrier by playing their defender, being an outlet, setting picks, cutting off picks, cutting backdoor, switching positions, and so on.

The 3-2-2 circle formation maintains a balanced attack and keeps the middle of the 8-meter arc clear for cutters.

The 3-2-2 Set

This is a basic offensive set. It offers good support for the ball, opens up the 8-meter arc for cutting through, and supports the pass and pick away or pass and cut away.

Players use the circle formation to keep the field balanced and to lend strong support to the ball carrier. After a player passes, she cuts at her defender (to make the defender pay attention to her and not the ball) and goes to the opposite side of the field to set a pick (pass and cut away). The player who receives the pass should challenge to the cage into the space that is vacated by the passer and should then look to shoot or feed a teammate cutting off the pick that is set for her by the passer. The remaining off-ball players are moving to support the ball carrier, playing their defenders, balancing the field, and anticipating the movement of the ball and the development of the next scoring opportunity.

The 2-4-1 Set

This offensive set is effective for an offense with strong dodgers and players who set and use picks well.

The five outside players have lots of space to dodge, while the inside players work off each other, setting picks and creating space for the ball carrier. Even your youngest players can understand the concept of being a player outside or inside the 8-meter arc and work accordingly. The players on the outside and inside of the 8-meter arc are interchangeable. If a player on the inside sets a pick and finds herself on the outside of the 8-meter arc, then direct the attack to balance the set and send the closest player to the inside. The attacker who finds herself behind the cage is in a great spot to roll the crease, or dodge, draw a sliding defender from an inside player, and feed the ball to her teammate.

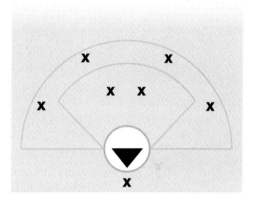

The 2-4-1 set is ideal for teams who set effective picks and whose attackers can handle the ball in tight when under pressure.

The Stack Set

In this set, the offense puts one or two feeders behind the goal (with the ball) while the remaining attackers stack themselves in a line or in a cluster usually at the top of the 8-meter arc.

The attackers cut out of the stack toward the goal, trying to get a quick step on a defender. Once a player cuts to the goal and the feeder doesn't use her, she fills back into the stack and cuts again. The feeder must be patient and accurate with her passes, and every so often she should try to move the ball back and forth behind the cage or challenge to the goal herself. The stack may be moved to either side of the 8-meter arc, and the feeders can feed from the wings (either side of the 8-meter arc) as well as from the top.

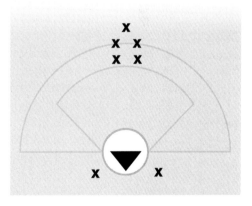

The stack set can catch a defender ball watching and allow her attacker to get a step on the defender with a quick cut to the cage.

These are just a few suggestions for setting up your team offense. It's up to you to determine which team offense is best for your players, and which will work the best for the type of defense you're playing against. When developing your team offense, do so without a lot of defensive pressure at first so that your attackers become familiar with the formations. *Gradually* increase the amount of defensive pressure to more gamelike conditions.

Clearing the Ball

Clearing the ball involves the entire team in an offensive situation. The idea is to use your player advantage (the goalie is key to successfully clearing the ball) to create open space to move the ball from defense to offense. Clearing the ball is the start of a team's attack on their opponent's goal. Clearing occurs whenever there's a change of possession in the defensive end of the field. There are settled and unsettled clearing situations. *Settled clearing* occurs when there are stoppages of play—after a pass or shot goes out-of-bounds, or after a foul is called. *Unsettled clearing* occurs when there's a quick change of possession, a loose ground ball, or a save. Each involves the same basic principles.

First, it's important for the team to recognize they're in a clearing situation. The goalie usually communicates this as she's giving direction to the defenders in her area, and they echo the information to the remaining field players. The goalie generally yells "Break!," "Get out!," or "Clear!" to alert her defenders. If the goalie has the ball inside her crease, she may hold it for up to 10 seconds and then must put the ball into play. Once your team gains possession in the defensive end of the field, it begins attacking your opponent's goal by moving the ball successfully upfield into the attacking end. A key component to clearing successfully is to maintain quality space between players throughout the entire clear. Once players bunch up it's easy for the defense to mark them, and if the ball carrier doesn't have sufficient space and passing options, she'll quickly get double-teamed. There are a number of options when clearing the ball.

Defensive movement during a clear.

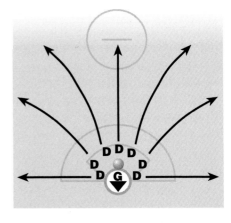

- The players *break out* in a balanced pattern, seeing the ball and maintaining good spacing, so that the goalie has a number of passing options.   **D9**
- The goalie looks to move the ball to the sideline first, avoiding the middle of the field in case of a turnover. Then the pass receiver looks to hit a cutter in the midfield or swings the ball to the opposite side of the field to avoid defensive pressure.
- If your goalie is capable, she clears the ball deep to a player on one side of the field around the 50-yard line to initiate a fast break (since the ball moves faster in the air than with a running player). This also gets the ball out of the defensive end quickly.
- The goalie clears the ball quickly to a defender who has cut laterally

Kathleen Geiger on Her Favorite Coach

Sue Stahl, coach of the U.S. World Cup team, never settled for anything but your best, and you knew she expected hard work. She wanted you to reach your potential and she gave you the tools, and you had to make it work.

Kathleen Geiger, Assistant Coach, U.S. World Cup
team, former World Cup player

along the goal line extended. The goalie can be an outlet for this defender if she draws pressure.

Questions and Answers

Q. My players are having trouble with the basics of catching and throwing. Should I move on to more advanced skills such as setting a pick?

A. The basic skills, like catching, throwing, and picking up ground balls, require the most time and attention. However, challenging your players (no matter what their level) with more advanced skills gives them the opportunity to improve and keeps them interested in the game.

Don't always expect your players to "get it" immediately. After you've thrown the challenging skill out there and let them have a go at it, move on to a skill you know they can accomplish.

CHAPTER 7

The Fundamentals of Defense

You've probably heard the saying "Offense wins games, defense wins championships." We believe this to be true and encourage you to stress proper individual and team defensive skills and concepts at every practice. It's the mission of the defense to prevent the offense from scoring. The defense does so by creating *defensive stops,* or situations where the defense has slowed down the offense and prevented a shot on goal. Successful team defense comes from fundamentally sound individual defense and solid communication skills.

There are primarily two kinds of defense, player-to-player and zone, which we'll discuss at the end of this chapter. There are three player-to-player systems—force weak all over the field, force away from the line of center, and force to the help. Each of these systems has strengths and weaknesses. It's important to determine which one your players will best understand and execute. The two zone systems—passive or sagging, and pressure—are more advanced concepts used at higher levels of play.

Defensive Positioning in the Midfield

Maintaining individual defensive positioning is a critical skill to teach young lacrosse players. Defenders are responsible for *marking* or *guarding* offensive players.

On-Ball Defense

The defender's objective is to prevent offensive players from scoring. Defenders also are responsible for creating a defensive stop, or an opportunity for the defense to gain possession of the ball through an interception, a block, a check, or a loose ground ball. On-ball defenders want to take something away from the ball carrier, such as a strong pass, a lane to the middle of the field, or a good angle from which to shoot. On-ball defenders can position themselves on the ball carrier's strong side and force her to pass or shoot with her weaker hand. Through well-executed individual defensive positioning, defenders can influence the movements of an offensive player with the ball by forcing her into a double team, away from the line of center, toward the sideline, or to a nondominant side. First we address on-ball defensive positioning in the midfield and then in a settled defense around the 8-meter arc.

Hip-to-hip positioning. When running with the ball carrier in the midfield or in transition, the defender should position herself to the side of the ball carrier, on the ball carrier's hip, with her shoulders almost square to the ball carrier.

The defender shouldn't position herself in front of the ball carrier because she wants to avoid running backward and allowing the ball carrier to easily beat her to open space. The defender shouldn't position herself behind the ball carrier because the ball carrier will cut her off to the open space in front of her, and the defender will end up chasing the ball carrier instead of dictating where she can go. Encourage your players to assess their opponents. One way to do this is to determine which hand is a player's strong hand. Defenders can force opponents to play with their weaker hand by positioning themselves properly. The defender should position her feet so they point in the same direction as the ball carrier's, slide her hand two-thirds of the way down her stick, and align herself alongside or slightly behind the ball carrier's hip as the ball carrier runs down the field. The defender should use her arms and hands to her advantage when playing hip-to-hip defense. She can extend her arms out and put her hands in front of the ball carrier (while still maintaining her balance) to help dictate the ball carrier's path and to slow her down. If a defender finds herself on her opponent's weak side (where she's forcing the opponent to use her strong hand), the defender should try to turn her player by stepping across her path

Left: A defender demonstrates outstanding defensive positioning with both her stick and body. Notice her top hand has slid down, and her weight is balanced.

Right: Notice that the defender's top hand has slid-down, and she is positioned on her attacker's hip during midfield play.

and forcing her to switch to her weak hand. The defender now has established her position on the ball carrier's strong side and is forcing her opponent to use her weak hand to pass and shoot.

Off-Ball Defense

As the ball carrier and her defender are moving down the field, the remaining defenders must position themselves accordingly, based on where the ball is and where opponents without the ball are. Generally, off-ball defenders want to position themselves goal-side, which means they are closer to the goal than their opponents. As a rule of thumb, the closer the defender and her opponent are to the ball carrier, the more tightly the defender should mark her opponent. If the ball carrier is farther away from the defender and her opponent, the defender can sag in toward her goal, meaning she drops to the top of the 8-meter closer to her goal. The defender should always have her stick up in the *passing lane,* an open space into which a cutter can move to receive a pass, and her top hand should be positioned about two-thirds of the way down the stick to increase her reach. An off-ball defender in the midfield should always watch the ball and the player she is marking so she must position herself at an angle to see both without having to turn her head.

Settled Defense

On-Ball Defensive Positioning

Defending an opponent with the ball in the midfield is different than defending an opponent with the ball in settled defense in front of the goal. In settled defense, the on-ball defender must stay low in her defensive stance, keep her stick up and in the passing lane, force the ball carrier where she wants this player to go (to a double team, away from the line of center, etc.), and communicate with her defensive teammates.

Footwork. Defenders must be able to quickly move forward, backward, and side to side while maintaining their balance. Adding footwork drills to your practices will greatly improve your players' ability to move in these directions while staying low and balanced.   **F1**   **F2**

The defensive stance. The on-ball defensive stance in women's lacrosse is similar to that used in basketball. The defender's feet should be shoulder-width apart, with the feet slightly offset; whether the left foot or right foot is in front depends on the defender's position on the field and the direction in which she is forcing the attacker to move. The defender's weight should be balanced on the balls of her feet, with her knees bent (she's almost in a seated position) and her back straight. The arms are away from the body, with the elbows slightly bent. The bottom hand is at the bottom of the stick, and the top hand is two-thirds of the way down. This allows the defender to remain balanced, to use her stick to dictate where the ball carrier can go, and to effectively cover the passing lanes. A defender should never play with her top hand at the very top of her stick because this limits her reach and throws her off-balance. A beginning player can choke up a bit with her top hand so she has complete control of the stick, but her hand shouldn't be all the way to the top.

As the ball carrier challenges to the cage, the defender doesn't want to back up into the 8-meter arc as the attacker approaches; this allows the attacker to get closer to the goal for a shot and doesn't take anything away from her.

Take something away. With their defensive stance, defenders want to take something away from the attackers and not concede a path to the goal. Teach your defenders to step up with either their left or right foot as the attacker challenges, which dictates to the attacker where the defender wants her to go. The on-ball defender must be listening for her teammates to tell her where the help is and must also listen for her goalie's directions. The goalie can see the offensive play developing; she's the main source of communication on defense.

Off-Ball Defensive Positioning

While one defender marks the player with the ball, six other defenders must be aware of what the ball carrier is doing and whether or not their teammate playing the ball needs help. In order to do this, the off-ball defenders must be able to see the ball and their particular opponent at the same time by assuming a correct angle between the two. Off-ball defenders want to avoid being in a position where they have to turn their head to see either the ball or their player. Remember, the attackers are taught to cut hard to the cage if they see the back of a defender's head. By maintaining a triangle between themselves, the ball, and their opponent, off-ball defenders can see both at the same time and react accordingly. In a settled defensive situation, ball-side defenders should have their backs facing the *line of center* (an imaginary line that splits the field in half from one center of the goal to the other), while defenders on the off-ball side should have their chests facing the line of center. This positioning encourages defenders to see both the ball and their player and discourages watching just the player.

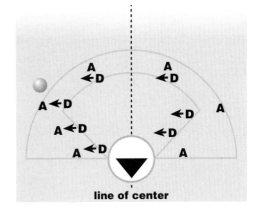

line of center

Defensive Slides

In settled defense, when the ball carrier looks to challenge her defender one-on-one to the cage, an adjacent off-ball defender slides to double-team the ball carrier. This leaves the second defender's player open, so the next adjacent defender must slide to cover the open player. The defenders continue

The line of center is an imaginary line from the center of one goal to the other that splits the field in half.

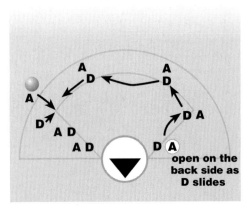

Defensive movement when the ball carrier challenges to the goal.

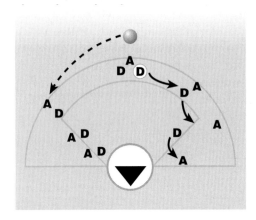

This defensive slide shows the defender sliding opposite to the way the ball moves.

sliding until one defender on the *back side* (the side opposite the ball) is left covering two offensive players.

Getting youth players to slide to double-team an opponent is hard enough, so expecting them to understand sliding to cover open players is too much, right? Wrong. Our feeling is you have to start somewhere, so why not teach your youngest players what it means to double-team the ball and slide to cover the open players? It may not be pretty at first, but as you implement the proper way to slide on defense in your drills at practice, your players will eventually execute those slides in games. **07**

When sliding to double-team, we teach our players to stay in the double team until they come up with the ball, or the ball gets passed. Once the ball is passed, the defensive unit must reset back into player-to-player defense. One way to reset is to have one of the defenders who was in the double team sprint to the middle of the 8-meter arc, toward the back side, where the open player should be. All the while, her teammates should be telling her where the open player is (see top diagram). Depending on where the double team ends up, this could be a very long slide.

Another, more advanced way to reset is to have the double-team defender who's opposite the way the ball moves slide to the next adjacent player and bump the remaining defenders around to the open player, making the slides a lot shorter (see bottom diagram). This method of resetting takes a lot of communication and anticipation on the part of the defenders, but it's extremely effective.

Double Teams

The purpose of a double team is to gain possession of the ball. The on-ball defender steps up to one side of the ball carrier at an angle and drives her toward another defender who's calling, "Bring her, bring her!" or "Double, double!" The second defender steps up to the other side of the ball carrier at an angle, which closes the double team. **D4**

The defenders' positions appear as if they are making a V with their feet and trapping the ball carrier between them. It's critical for the defenders to remain on the same sides during the double team; otherwise they'll end up cutting each other off as the attacker tries to get out of the double team. Each defender has a specific responsibility in a double team. One defender holds solid body position while the other defender tries to stick-check the ball carrier and dislodge the ball. Throughout the double team the defenders should be communicating what they're doing by saying, "I've got hold . . . I'm holding!" and "I've got check . . . I'm checking!" The pressure of a double team alone may force the attacker to drop the ball, make a bad pass, or hang (lower) her stick enough for a solid stick check. The defenders in the double-team situation want the ball and must stay with the double team until they gain possession or until the attacker moves the ball. Once the ball is passed, one defender must stay on the opponent while the other defender resets back into the settled defensive system, looking for the open player. Her defensive teammates should be telling her where the open player is—most likely she'll be on the back side, the side of the field opposite the ball.

Two defenders close a double team. Notice the V-shape of the defenders' feet formed by proper positioning. The right-side defender is holding while the left defender attempts a check.

Defending a Cut through the 8-Meter Arc

Off-ball defenders don't want to allow cutters to move easily through the 8-meter arc. Whether you're coaching youth lacrosse or working with collegiate-level players, defending off-ball cutters through the 8-meter arc is an important technique to practice. Too often defenders are content to follow attackers as they cut for the ball, and they find themselves trailing the cutters. Teach off-ball defenders to step up into the path of the cutter, forcing her to go around the defender and changing the path of her cut. Stepping up and squaring her hips to the cutter allows the defender to disrupt the cut, slow down the attacker, and gain good body position. Defenders want to avoid opening up their hips and giving the attacker an open lane for cutting. This is a difficult concept for youth players to understand and is best taught without sticks at first.

Player-to-Player Defense

The general concept behind player-to-player defense is that each defensive player is responsible for a player on the opposing team. The on-ball defender must be able to contain her player when she's challenging to the cage until a defensive teammate can slide to help. Off-ball defenders must position themselves at the appropriate angles so they can see both the ball and their player. All defenders must communicate clearly and consistently. Within team defense, the individual defenders want to position themselves *ball-side* (between their opponent and the ball) and *goal-side* (between their opponent and the goal). This allows the defenders to cover both the passing lanes as well as the lanes to the goal. Defenders should always have their sticks up

---

Heather Dow on Her Favorite Coach

Sue Stahl, the coach of the U.S. World Cup team, is tough and demanding because she wants as many kids as possible to experience the self-satisfaction that comes from striving for and achieving a dream. She recognizes that as a teacher of the game of lacrosse she has a responsibility to the whole person, not just the athlete, so she nurtures individual and team character, sportsmanship, and the realization that no matter how fiercely we compete, ultimately lacrosse is a game to be enjoyed.

Heather Dow, former U.S. World Cup team goalie

---

and in the passing lanes. They should slide their top hand at least two-thirds of the way down their stick so they can cover as much space as possible and use their stick to direct the path of the offensive player. Here are three useful player-to-player systems.

Force Weak All over the Field

This defensive system relies on a defender establishing a defensive body position that will force the ball carrier to her weak hand no matter where she is on the offensive end of the field. Off-ball defenders also establish a defensive body position, taking away the strong-hand cuts to the ball and forcing the attackers to use their weaker hand to catch, pass, and shoot. This is a more advanced defensive system that requires quick, aggressive defenders and the ability to determine your opponent's strong hand.

Force Away from the Line of Center

This defensive system is most appropriate for 6- to 12-year-old players. Draw an imaginary line down the middle of the field through both goals (the line of center). Depending on what side the ball is on, the on-ball defender steps up and takes away the middle of the field, forcing the ball carrier down and away from the goal, thus minimizing the angle with which the attacker can shoot.

Force to the Help

This defensive system relies on the on-ball defender's ability to force the ball carrier *to the help,* or toward the majority of her fellow defenders, who can then look to double-team. The help may be over the top of the 8-meter arc into the center, or it may be down the side away from the line of center.

Zone Defense

Zone defense is rarely executed at the youth level but can be effective if your players have a solid understanding of zone concepts. In zone defense defenders cover areas (zones) on the field and not individual players. A defender covers an attacker who moves into her zone but releases the attacker once that player moves out of her area or zone. When running a zone defense, players must be aware of the 3-second rule.

CHAPTER 8

The Practice

A clamoring group of 6- and 7-year-old girls swarms around you as you get out of your car, only a few minutes late: "Can I be goalie?" "Can I be center?" "When do we scrimmage?" "I forgot my water bottle!" "Do you have an extra mouth guard?" "Where are the balls?"

Here you are, already behind and feeling a little overwhelmed as you attempt to get your first practice going. There's not a moment to banter with the eighteen individuals who crave your undivided attention. In fact, there's no time to say more than "Hey! Where's the goal cage? Does everyone have a ball?" High-stress, counterproductive, disheveled: this isn't the way you wanted to start the season. These are not happy times.

Here are some tips for starting off on the right foot and organizing your season.

Preparation Is the Key
Arrive Early

Arrive at the practice site at least 15 minutes before the scheduled start of practice. It's a golden time to develop one-on-one relationships with players and parents who straggle in early, as well as to set up the field for practice. Practice time, limited as it is, needs to be devoted to developing your players' skills and shouldn't be used for moving goal cages, fixing nets, lining the field, or positioning cones, etc. Try to get these things out of the way ahead of time. (You can have your Assistant Coach of the Day—see next page— help you prepare the field.)

When the field is ready, take a few moments to review your practice plan and roster and gather your thoughts as you mingle with players and parents. Take a deep breath—or several—to get settled and composed. Assess the weather, and if it looks like storms are approaching, ask parents to stand by. Rain won't hurt anyone, but have a plan of action in case of lightning or high winds.

Establish an Assistant Coach of the Day

Make sure that no time will be wasted sitting around. Personally put a ball into the pocket of each arriving player and instruct her to start stick-work tricks. Now is a perfect opportunity to designate one of the players as an Assistant Coach of the Day. Pull her aside and congratulate her, citing some positive aspect of her play or personality. Tell her she has been chosen to lead the stretching activity as well as help you set up the field. Suggest a few stretches for her to announce to the team when it's time to do so and assist her by demonstrating the stretches. This probably will be a fun and much-anticipated honor for most girls, but maybe not for all. Assure shy players that you're there to help them. If a girl vehemently protests that she doesn't want to be Assistant Coach of the Day, tell her you respect her wishes and hope she'll reconsider when you ask her again later on in the season.

Start on Time

If practice is supposed to start at 4 P.M., then right at 4 be ready to blow your whistle and have the girls "Bring it in." Discipline, structure, and consistency are critical, especially for young beginners. If you don't begin practice until the last few teammates straggle in, a lackadaisical attitude will trickle down and infect the team. A routine of being organized and starting promptly promotes a positive and respectful environment and gives credibility to your authority as coach.

As important as structure is, there also needs to be a fair degree of flexibility built in. If you put a drill out there and notice that either the girls aren't getting it or key players are missing, by all means make a change. Improvise with an alternate drill that teaches a similar concept.

Take Notes

To keep yourself on task, treat yourself to a new spiral-bound notebook in which you'll devote about a page per practice to record your plan, including drills, thoughts, Monday-morning quarterbacking, and notes to yourself about former and future practices. Write down everything: thoughts about how Joanie is doing at attack as well as personal reminders ("ask Sue about her mom's recent surgery"). Keep a running, updated list of phone numbers and e-mail addresses so it's easy to contact the opposing coach about a game that needs rescheduling and alert an umpire about the change, as well as to keep the league commissioner up-to-date about equipment needs ("a throat protector is missing from our goalie equipment") and field issues ("the goal cage has a rip in the netting").

It's a common error to get stuck doing one thing and thus get only one thing accomplished, letting lots of other drills and skill-building tactics fall by the wayside. By routinely shrugging off plans and thinking, "Oh, I'll get to that another day," you'll find yourself with a team that's ill-prepared for their first game. If you stay on task, it'll help your players to do the same.

The Best-Laid Plans

No matter how organized you are, thunderstorms happen; injuries happen; and stomach viruses happen—all too fast. Perhaps a third of your team doesn't show up in time for the opening draw of a game because of a bus breakdown on the way home from a school field trip.

The key to capably handling the unforeseen circumstances that inevitably crop up in the course of every lacrosse season is to have backup plans. At the very least, mentally walk yourself through the what-ifs, if only in a general sense. In the event of bad weather: Is there an indoor site? Could all the kids crowd into your car? In the event of an emergency: Can you count on the coolheadedness of your assistant coach or parent helpers? Or another coach on a nearby field?

When presented with dilemmas, keep this simple question in mind as a guide. Ask yourself what you, as a parent, would expect or want a coach to do if it were your child in a similar situation—if your child were throwing up or if your child twisted an ankle. Don't hesitate to call whoever is listed on the child's lacrosse player profile form as an emergency contact.

You are responsible for these kids as an adult supervisor, not just as a coach. You can always tell your other players to do stick-work tricks for 10 minutes while you tend to an unwell or injured player. If a player needs to use a bathroom during practice—the one nearest to our home field is a portable toilet across a country road and on the edge of a distant wood—be sure to send her with a buddy-escort or, better yet, a parent-escort from the sideline. Don't let a player venture alone into otherwise empty school buildings. Above all, you want to provide a safe and nurturing environment where they are comfortable enough to take risks, challenge themselves, and test limits.

The All-Important First Practice

This is the moment to set the tone, establish rapport, and exude authority. You do this first by welcoming players and parents as important parts of the team; after all, there wouldn't be a team without them! It's a watershed moment in many girls' sports careers—the very first experience with a coach for some—and you can help determine whether they'll return with smiling enthusiasm or perhaps not return at all.

The first practice can be extremely intimidating for young players. Get to know them as individuals right away and address them by their first name. At some point during the practice, approach each and every player individually and make a positive comment to her using her first name: "Sarah! That was a terrific ground ball pickup!" or "Nice cradle, Jane!" It's absolutely critical for a young person meeting an authority figure to feel like she's been noticed and appreciated.

Time for a name game: Throughout the first couple of practices, blow your whistle occasionally and stand next to a player, asking: "OK, everybody,

---

Team-Building Ideas

The Buddy System

When you first meet your bright-eyed group of eighteen to twenty lacrosse players, you can immediately start to foster a sense of camaraderie and acceptance by instituting a buddy system. Each player is assigned a buddy. If you're somewhat familiar with your players and feel comfortable about assigning a more experienced player with a newcomer, or a bolder one with a shy one, this may help break down some communication barriers. If not, we've also seen success by simply allowing the girls to pick their own buddies. Besides cheering for the team as a whole, buddies give extra boosts of support to each other, on and off the field. You can quickly pair up your team for drills by saying, "OK, get with your buddies." You can also assign fun things to foster friendships: "Tell me one special thing you've found out about your buddy."

---

who's this?" Your players will yell out their teammate's name, helping each other as well as you and your assistants and parents become better acquainted.

General Practice Format

Establishing a practice routine is important for you and your players. A practice routine provides structure and helps players (and coaches) establish good practice habits. We recommend following the same basic routine for each practice no matter what level (beginner, intermediate, or advanced) your players are, but vary the activities, difficulty of drills, number of players, player combinations, space, and concepts presented to keep players motivated and interested. A Practice Planner (see pages 88–89) is an excellent way to keep your practices on task and organized. These planners outline a 90-minute practice that can be used for beginner, intermediate, and advanced players. A 90-minute practice is the maximum for beginner and intermediate players, and a 2-hour practice is the maximum for advanced players.

Put a ball in the pocket of each arriving player and tell her to warm up either individually or with a partner; suggest passing, ground ball pickups, and stick-work tricks.

Bring It In (5 minutes)

Greet the players and let them know with enthusiasm about the format for practice for the day; tell them what you're trying to accomplish as a team; outline drills and activities that are going to be worked on. Let them know you'll call three water breaks over the next 90 minutes, at regular intervals. Players probably will attempt to interject comments and questions. Some may view your opening huddle as a social gathering to discuss the weekend. Keep them on task. The coach does the talking now, emphasizing the focus of the practice and explaining the warm-up activity. The team breaks from Bring it In with Give a Shout.

Warm-Up (maximum 10 minutes)

Raise your players' body temperature a couple degrees with activities that develop and benefit their lacrosse skills and game abilities. These warm-ups should be designed to build interest and enthusiasm and set the tone for practice. Activities should emphasize body control and encourage quick thinking. Any types of tag or chasing games—players pursuing each other—are good warm-up options. The emphasis should be on fun and movement.

Stretching (5 minutes)

Stretching is essential for all players, but for different reasons. It allows players to connect as a team. It's an ideal time for players to develop leadership roles and the ability to communicate with teammates. Your Assistant Coach of the Day can lead this activity. Be sure to include stretches for the legs, midsection, arms, shoulders, and neck. It's always a good idea to consult a doctor, trainer, or other appropriate resource to determine what stretches would best benefit young female lacrosse players.

FUN-damentals (25 minutes)

A big chunk of each practice should be devoted to fundamental drills and skill building. There are five key components to keeping this part of practice fun, lively, and effective.

- keep the players moving
- break players into small groups
- use stations
- emphasize one key skill at each station
- insist on repetition

It's no surprise that a foundation of solid skills is essential to the growth and development of young lacrosse players. The basis for any athlete's success is how well she executes the fundamentals. Equally important is understanding how to transfer those fundamental skills to gamelike situations. Fundamental drills provide terrific opportunities to teach and correct your players. As best you can, minimize the amount of time players spend standing around. Divide the players into small-sided situations—groups of twos and threes instead of long lines of eight players or more. When executing fundamentals, a terrific way to keep practice moving is to set up *stations*, different areas of the field that concentrate on specific skills. You and your assistant coaches can spend a certain number of minutes monitoring each station to ensure that the small groups of girls keep moving through the particular activity at each station and then rotate to the next station. Don't let the kids just go through the same old motions. Walk around while they're in their stations and try to comment about

The most important thing to remember when picking up a ground ball is to run through it.

Practice Planner

Bring it in (5 min.):

_____
_____
_____
_____
_____

Warm-up (max. 10 min.):

_____
_____
_____
_____

Stretching (5 min.):

_____
_____
_____
_____

FUN-damentals (25 min.):

_____
_____
_____
_____
_____

Offensive-defensive combinations/game concepts (20 min.):

_____
_____
_____

Scrimmage play/game concepts (20 min.):

_____
_____
_____

Bring it in/wrap-up/stretching (5 min.):

_____
_____
_____
_____

Practice Planner

Bring it in (5 min.):

Welcome.
Discuss practice objectives: work on ground balls, introduce new shooting drill emphasizing outside shots, work on player-up situations
Give a shout to start practice

Warm-up (max. 10 min.):

Flag Tag: emphasize change of direction, moving into open space.

Stretching (5 min.):

Stretch legs and arms

FUN-damentals (25 min.):

Stick-work tricks (5 min.), Partner Passing (10 min.)
— emphasize stepping into the pass,
Star Shooting (10 min.),
— emphasize shooting with power

Offensive-defensive combinations/game concepts (20 min.):

Teach three-on-two Concepts
— positioning and practice

Scrimmage play/game concepts (20 min.):

Half-field Scrimmage — put players in three-on-two situations; stop play to discuss proper spacing.

Bring it in/wrap-up/stretching (5 min.):

Review observations at practice, remind players of next practice day and time, compliment them on effort

Give a shout!

Now You're Thinking

One highly effective coaching tool is to allow players to discover the components of a skill or drill or game concept that you're trying to teach by asking them questions and encouraging them to think on their own. This way they're more likely to retain the information you need them to remember.

For instance, you demonstrate picking up a stationary ground ball for your team. Instead of talking them through it with a long-winded explanation detailing all the various components of the skill, ask questions instead: Where should I position myself to pick up this ground ball? Why? What are my legs doing as I approach? What are they doing as I pick it up? Do I stop or keep moving, and why? What do I do with the ball once it's in my stick? The girls will be eager to answer your questions. Guide them so that you pull out of them exactly what you're looking for. The Now You're Thinking method involves everyone by getting all the players into a mind-set of concentrating on what's happening in front of them. When they discover for themselves that their knees need to be bent and their knuckles need to scrape the ground during a ground ball pickup, they'll remember it better than if you told it to them a dozen times. Reiterate "Now you're thinking!" and "You've got it!" Praise them for their participation.

something to each player. This is prime teaching time; demonstrate and correct so they can improve.

Set up a station of stick-work tricks, a station with one-on-ones (where girls work on individual attack and defensive skills), and a dodging station. On another day you might set up a station for contested ground balls, a station for shooting, and another for passing (a quick-moving shuttle). Spend a moment at each station touching on a key teaching point—one key teaching point for each particular situation. For instance, to the girls at the dodging station, you might say, "Remember to lead with that stick coming out of the dodge." To those doing one-on-ones: "Defensively, keep sticks straight up and down, not across the body so we're not fouling." And to stick-work tricksters: "Switch from your dominant hand to your nondominant hand, from left to right. Use both hands!"

The repetition of fundamental drills will help your girls develop good basic skills and form good habits at the same time.

Offensive and Defensive Combinations/Game Concepts (15 to 20 minutes)

It's of no use to your girls to master the fundamental skills of lacrosse if they can't then transfer these basics into gamelike situations. That step requires your players to call on practice experiences in order to make decisions and execute skills in games and scrimmages. If you focus only on developing fundamental skills, then your girls will fall short on being able to put them into action on game day. In addition to learning the basics, players need to be encouraged to figure out for themselves and their team the best plans of attack, or the best ways to defend. How, as a coach, do you help them achieve a conceptual perspective of lacrosse? The first step is to put them in small-sided, gamelike situations.

One of the most important—and challenging—concepts to teach is creating space for the ball carrier. The natural inclination is for all the girls on the field to run toward the ball, excitedly calling their teammate's name and waving their stick, and then hover near her in a big clump. In a three-on-three or four-on-four station within your practice, begin focusing on good field sense by developing an understanding of creating space. Field players need to learn when to support the ball and how. They need to recognize when the ball carrier has a good opportunity to go to the cage and allow her to do so—and perhaps support her by going behind the cage to chase down a missed shot. The fewer people in this drill initially, the greater chance of more lightbulbs being turned on: this is when your players have the best chance to "get it." Once they do, then you can progress to five-on-fives, six-on-sixes, and finally, seven-on-sevens. Then you can throw in more variables.

Scrimmage Play/Game Concepts (20 minutes)

Now it's time to transfer the offensive and defensive concepts into game situations while scrimmaging. Scrimmaging is a great treat. Whether it's a half- or full-field scrimmage, it's a fun activity in which everyone gets involved. This is your chance as a coach to really assess your players. Stand back and let them play. Just observe. Start them off with clear direction and enthusiastic compliments. Then, just watch for that first practice or two to see what you have. It'll become apparent in scrimmages who has a natural sense of the field and play. You'll be able to determine which players hide and are afraid of the ball. You'll notice connections emerging between teammates. You'll recognize who is competitive and aggressive, and who is reserved. Stress *effort*: remind the girls to hustle after ground balls, to cut hard for the ball, to pay attention to the action. Let one side win and the other lose. Not everything can be a tie. Kids need to recognize they'll win some and lose some, and they can learn to do both with dignity.

Even if the girls scrimmage for just 10 minutes, always have a halftime during which you pull them in, encourage them to have a drink to stay hydrated, and offer a few key points based on your observations. Some coaches blow the kids away with too much information and too many directions. Focus on two or three key points for them to keep in mind when they go back out and finish the scrimmage. It's important for your whole team to realize that when you're talking to one individual, you're really addressing everyone. You may be talking to one player about a particular skill or technique, but everyone should be listening at that time: "Caroline, I noticed you were dropping your stick to your hip a lot in that first half when on defense. I'd like to see you keep that stick a little more straight up and down in the passing lanes. And the rest of the defenders should keep that in mind also."

When you're giving instruction remind players that it's not a time for two-way conversation. The coach is the sole authority figure at practice. When you ask them to do something, the responses should be limited to

It's important for coaches to interact individually with their players.

"OK, Coach" or "I don't understand, Coach." It's far too easy to waste a quarter of an hour debating with a 7-year-old about why she missed a particular shot.

Variety is the spice of life with youth players. Don't call for a full-field scrimmage at the end of every practice. Mix it up. Be creative. Set up a little tournament: break up twenty players into five-on-fives and have the winners play and the losers play. You don't necessarily need goals; use cones.

Remember that energy levels are probably highest at the beginning of practices. By midpractice, energy and enthusiasm may wane. Scrimmaging and competitive drills are a good way to infuse energy into the ends of practices.

When you offer a comment about a scrimmage, express constructive criticisms first—perhaps two things you want to see fixed next time—and then end with a positive comment, a compliment. Let them hear the good stuff last so they can walk away happy—knowing what they have to work on but bolstered with the feeling that the coach noticed what they did well.

A final tip: Force the kids to use their nondominant hand during scrimmaging, even if it's just for 2 minutes. Switching hands is often forgotten in gamelike situations. Don't let something you've worked hard on in fundamentals get neglected in scrimmages. Give your players the confidence to use their nondominant hand in game situations.

Bring It In/Wrap-Up/Stretching (5 minutes)

During practice, you are the authority, and the players are the listeners. However, it's important that you're not always the one doing all the talking. It's important to congratulate them on lots of hustle and good effort (if this was the case). Then ask them, "What did you do well as a team today?" Ask them a question that will allow them to revisit something positive. Give them ownership of success, of accomplishment. "What did you like about today's practice?" "What did we achieve today as a team?"

You should feel free to elaborate on the girls' answers. It helps to build their trust and establishes a line of communication between you and the players. You may want to ask: "Did anyone have any trouble today in practice?" When you ask your players for feedback, you'll be surprised at what you'll get out of them.

Occasionally you might inquire if anyone is hurt in any way: "Is everyone feeling good? Is everyone really tired?" Their responses will help you gauge the intensity level of the next practice.

Wrap up by giving your players some idea about what the next practice will be like: "We spent a lot of time on the offensive drills today. Next Tuesday our emphasis will be on defense." Remind them about the time and place of the next practice, and tell them when the next game is scheduled.

At the end of the practice, challenge them to do everyday things with their nondominant hand: hold a fork, brush their hair and teeth, set the table, reach for the car door, write a letter, unzip their jacket. Tell them you want to hear about all the things they can do with their weaker hand. The more they use their nondominant hand in everyday life, the easier it will be to handle their stick.

Water breaks. Keep your players hydrated. The rule of thumb is that if they're thirsty, they're already becoming dehydrated. Build regular water breaks into practices: two is usually sufficient, but have three if it's really hot. Players should provide their own water bottles.

Stretching. As you're asking your end-of-practice questions, do it in the context of a 5-minute stretching routine. Encourage the girls to get in a circle with all eyes on you, so they're stretching while you're talking.

Conclude every practice with Give a Shout.

As a coach, you should not leave the practice site until every child has been picked up. You are responsible for their safety and well-being while they're in your care. As you're gathering equipment, keep an eye on those players leaving with parents and, more important, on those not leaving.

Sample Practices

This section provides customized practices for a four-week period (the length of a typical recreation girls' lacrosse preseason) and is designed to make your first experience as "the coach" organized and painless.

These practices are based on a 90-minute time frame and can be used with (or modified to fit) beginner-, intermediate-, or advanced-level youth players. For example, if you have a group of 6- to 8-year-old players who are new to lacrosse, place more emphasis on teaching and developing their fundamental skills. With a more advanced group of 11- to 12-year-olds, more emphasis might be placed on the offensive and defensive combination drills and the development of game strategies.

You may choose to shorten or lengthen your practices based on the age and skill level of your team. As you plan future practices, use these as templates, mixing and matching a variety of drills from chapters 10, 11, and 12. Keep your practices moving by setting up stations so as many players as possible are touching the ball or learning new techniques. These practices are a gift from us to you. (We only wish someone had done this for us!) They'll give you a much-needed head start in coaching girls' lacrosse. Enjoy!

Drill/Activity	Objective/Suggestion	Time
Sample Practice #1 for Week 1 (90 minutes)		
Bring it in	Gather the team to discuss practice plans for the day	5 min.
Flag Tag F2	Warm up.	5 min.
	Stretch legs, arms, shoulders, neck, and midsection. Assistant Coach for the Day leads stretching.	5 min.
Assorted stick-work tricks	To improve stick handling.	5 min.
Partner Passing F12	Fundamental skills.	5 min.
Work-the-Point Passing F14	Fundamental skills.	6 min.
Ground Ball Blob Passing F22	Fundamental skills.	9 min.
Teach the hot spots, positions 1, 2, 3, 4, 5, and 6, etc.	Set up players in front of the goal to demonstrate.	5 min.
Shooting Shuttle F29		7 min.
Triple Shot F27		7 min.
Water break		2 min.
Continuous One-on-One to Goal O1	Offensive-defensive combinations: teach one-on-one and two-on-two concepts at stations when possible.	10 min.
Water break		2 min.
Half-field scrimmage	Teach offensive and defensive concepts.	10 min.
Water break		2 min.
Bring it in/wrap-up/stretching	Closing remarks, cooldown, stretching.	5 min.
Sample Practice #2 for Week 1 (90 minutes)		
Bring it in	Gather the team to discuss practice plans for the day.	5 min.
Fast Feet F1	Warm up.	5 min.
	Stretch legs, arms, shoulders, neck, and midsection. Assistant Coach for the Day leads stretching.	5 min.
Stick-work tricks	To improve stick handling.	5 min.
Partner Passing F12	Fundamental skills.	5 min.
Triples F13	Fundamental skills.	7 min.
Four Corners with a Shot F31	Fundamental skills.	8 min.
Water break		2 min.
Continuous One-on-One to Goal O1	Offensive-defensive combinations: teach one-on-ones at stations when possible.	15 min.
Box Double Team D4	To teach double-teaming.	9 min.
Water break		2 min.
Half-field scrimmage	Teach offensive and defensive concepts.	15 min.
Water break	Halfway through scrimmage.	2 min.
Bring it in/wrap-up/stretching	Closing remarks, cooldown, stretching.	5 min.

Drill/Activity	Objective/Suggestion	Time
Sample Practice #1 for Week 2 (90 minutes)		
Bring it in	Gather the team to discuss practice plans for the day.	5 min.
Fast Feet F1	Warm up.	5 min.
Grab-a-Ball Tag F3	Warm up.	5 min.
Center Draw O8	Warm up.	5 min.
	Stretch legs, arms, shoulders, neck, and midsection. Assistant Coach for the Day leads stretching.	5 min.
Stick-work tricks	To improve stick handling.	5 min.
Partner Passing F12	Fundamental skills.	5 min.
Three in One F19	Fundamental skills.	6 min.
Blob Passing F16	Fundamental skills.	7 min.
Water break		1 min.
Cross the Line D8	Work on stepping up on defense.	10 min.
Offensive Three-on-Two to Goal O2 and Defending the Three-on-Two D5	Offensive-defensive combinations: teach three-on-twos at stations when possible for lots of repetitions both ways.	15 min.
Mark-Up D3	To work on defensive marking up.	10 min.
Water break	Halfway through Mark-Up.	1 min.
Bring it in/wrap-up/stretching	Closing remarks, cooldown, stretching.	5 min.
Sample Practice #2 for Week 2 (90 minutes)		
Bring it in	Gather the team to discuss practice plans for the day.	5 min.
Flag Tag F2	Warm up.	5 min.
	Stretch legs, arms, shoulders, neck, and midsection. Assistant Coach for the Day leads stretching.	5 min.
Stick-work tricks; Center Draw O8 for drawers	To improve stick handling.	5 min.
Square Passing F15	Fundamental skills.	5 min.
Pass-Back Weave F17	Fundamental skills.	10 min.
Water break		1 min.
Competitive Ground Balls to Goal F21	Fundamental skills.	5 min.
Offensive Three-on-Two to Goal O2 , Defending the Three-on-Two D5 , and Breakout O5	Offensive-defensive combinations: teach three-on-twos at stations when possible for lots of repetitions both ways.	20 min.
Water break		2 min.
Full-field scrimmage	Teach offensive and defensive concepts.	20 min.
Water break	Halfway through scrimmage.	2 min.
Bring it in/wrap-up/stretching	Closing remarks, cooldown, stretching.	5 min.

(continued next page)

Drill/Activity	Objective/Suggestion	Time
Sample Practice #1 for Week 3 (90 minutes)		
Bring it in	Gather the team to discuss practice plans for the day.	5 min.
Fast Feet F1	Warm up.	5 min.
	Stretch legs, arms, shoulders, neck, and midsection. Assistant Coach for the Day leads stretching.	5 min.
Stick-work tricks	To improve stick handling.	5 min.
Partner Passing F12	Fundamental skills.	5 min.
Partner Dodging F23	Fundamental skills.	5 min.
Five-on-Five Dodging Box F25	Fundamental skills.	5 min.
Water break		1 min.
Star Shooting F28	Fundamental skills.	10 min.
Ground Ball Tag F20	To work on ground balls.	10 min.
Defensive Clearing D9	Set up the clearing pattern to teach clearing the ball.	10 min.
Water break		2 min.
Half-Field Scramble O7	Offensive-defensive combinations: use stations when possible. Use seven-on-seven to work on defensive slides.	15 min.
Water break	Halfway through Half-Field Scramble.	2 min.
Bring it in/wrap-up/stretching	Closing remarks, cooldown, stretching.	5 min.
Sample Practice #2 for Week 3 (90 minutes)		
Bring it in	Gather the team to discuss practice plans for the day.	5 min.
Grab-a-Ball Tag F3	Warm up.	5 min.
	Stretch legs, arms, shoulders, neck, and midsection. Assistant Coach for the Day leads stretching.	5 min.
Stick-work tricks	To improve stick handling.	5 min.
Triples F13	Fundamental skills.	5 min.
Pass-Back Weave F17	Fundamental skills.	7 min.
Competitive Ground Balls F21	Fundamental skills.	7 min.
Lead with Your Head F30	Fundamental skills.	7 min.
Shooting Shuttle F29	Fundamental skills.	7 min.
Water break		1 min.
Offensive Four-on-Three to Goal O3 , Defending the Four-on-Three D6 , Offensive Five-on-Four to Goal O4 , and Defending the Five-on-Four D7	Offensive-defensive combinations: use stations when possible.	20 min.
Water break		1 min.
Full-field scrimmage	Teach offensive and defensive concepts.	10 min.
Bring it in/wrap-up/stretching	Closing remarks, cooldown, stretching.	5 min.

Drill/Activity	Objective/Suggestion	Time
Sample Practice #1 for Week 4 (90 minutes)		
Bring it in	Gather the team to discuss practice plans for the day.	5 min.
Flag Tag F2	Warm up.	5 min.
	Stretch legs, arms, shoulders, neck, and midsection. Assistant Coach for the Day leads stretching.	5 min.
Stick-work tricks	To improve stick handling.	5 min.
Blob Passing F16	Fundamental skills.	6 min.
Three in One F19	Fundamental skills.	5 min.
Four Corners with a Shot F31	Fundamental skills.	10 min.
Water break		1 min.
Cross the Line D8	To work on defensive slides.	5 min.
Box Double Team D4	Fundamental skills.	7 min.
Half-Field Scramble O7	Offensive-defensive combinations: use stations when possible.	15 min.
Water break		1 min.
Set up free position shots (8 meters) to the goal (see pages 32–33).	To work on 8-meter play at two cages (lots of repetitions).	15 min.
Bring it in/wrap-up/stretching	Closing remarks, cooldown, stretching.	5 min.
Sample Practice #2 for Week 4 (90 minutes)		
Bring it in	Gather the team to discuss practice plans for the day.	5 min.
Grab-a-Ball Tag F3	Warm up.	5 min.
	Stretch legs, arms, shoulders, neck, and midsection. Assistant Coach for the Day leads stretching.	5 min.
Stick-work tricks	To improve stick handling.	5 min.
Triples F13	Fundamental skills.	5 min.
Pass-Back Weave F17	Fundamental skills.	12 min.
Competitive Ground Balls F21	Fundamental skills.	10 min.
Water break		1 min.
Center Draw O8	To work on center draw play.	5 min.
Full-field scrimmage	Work on game-day procedures and address offensive and defensive full-field concepts.	30 min.
Water break	Halfway through scrimmage.	2 min.
Bring it in/wrap-up/stretching	Closing remarks, cooldown, stretching.	5 min.

Kara Ariza Cooke on Her Favorite Coach

Kathleen Geiger, assistant coach of the U.S. World Cup team, elevated both my game and the interest I had in the sport during my ninth grade season. Her enthusiasm and love of the game were (and still are) both motivating and contagious.   Kara Ariza Cooke, U.S. World Cup team member

Specialty Practices

The Practice after a Tough Loss

Well, it happens to the best of us. Your team was moving along just fine, winning some games, losing some games (only by a couple of goals), and then it happens: you get smashed!

How do you handle the practice after a tough loss: either a demoralizing loss by 20 goals, or a devastating loss by 1 goal in the last 10 seconds? One thing's for sure—you don't dwell on it! Come to the next practice with lots of energy; don't let your players rehash the experience over and over. Assess the areas where your team needs to perform better. Was it a lack of possession? Did your defense slide to double-team? Was it poor shooting? Were you able to slow the ball down at all? Were you just completely outmatched? These are some of the questions you want to ask yourself, and then it's time to practice! When you Bring it In, highlight some of the things you want to work on at practice, let the team know what adjustments were necessary in the game, and assure them that with a little hard work, they will improve. Mention some positive accomplishments in the game to let the team know you noticed. Talk to them about inevitable stumbling blocks in life and how the tough loss was an experience to learn from. Enthusiastically Give a Shout and start your warm-up.

Defensive drills should be the focus for the practice after a good drubbing. Set up drills to work on slowing down the ball in transition, sliding to double-team, marking cutters in the 8-meter arc, and picking up ground balls.

The Practice after a Big Win

Well done, Coach! You beat your opponent by nine goals, the team played well, and everybody's feeling great. Let's keep up the good work. The practice following a big win is not the time to slack off. It's time to polish. Build on your offense's success by incorporating additional shooting drills into that next practice. Continue to challenge your defense by putting them in player-down situations; tell them what a great job they did holding their opponents to a couple of goals. Remind your team that they can't afford to get comfortable after a big win; the focus still needs to be on consistent daily improvement.

The Practice after a Poor Shooting Performance

Your offense couldn't hit the broad side of a barn during the last game, much less the inside of the goal cage. What to do? *Keep shooting!* The practice after a poor shooting performance should be completely dedicated to shooting and offensive drills. Get your team back on track. Put them in drills that allow them to score. Start without a goalie so your team has no trouble finding the net. Give them targets to shoot at: put a pinny in each corner of the goal cage and have a contest to see who has the most accurate shot. Set up shooting stations so your entire team is getting lots of touches on the ball.

The Stick-Doctor Party

Players who understand how to string and unstring lacrosse sticks are affectionately known as stick doctors. Some players take great pride in their abilities to string sticks. We feel it's important for players to understand how a stick is put together, how to best tighten it, and how to work in a legal pocket: essentially, how to break in a stick sooner rather than later. We recommend a team party or get-together—it can be as simple as a half-hour special session before practice, or it can be a more organized party at a player's or coach's house.

The object is to take a women's lacrosse stick—perhaps an extra that you have—and let the kids see you (or perhaps a local stick doctor from a lacrosse equipment store) take it apart, untying and retying the knots to loosen and tighten the pocket. Teach them how to repair a stick if one of the strings breaks. Completely disassemble one stick, taking the pocket out of the stick head, and let the girls have a hand in restringing that particular stick.

To really get everyone involved and make your party more fun, encourage the girls to customize their sticks, whether with stickers or tape or permanent markers, or perhaps paint or nail polish. Sticks allow the girls to express themselves as individuals. Ideally, a girl's stick needs to fit her personality as well as fit her body.

Have your girls compare and contrast their sticks, many of which may be very different. Suggest to your players that their sticks are not only valuable and personal pieces of athletic equipment, but also extensions of their very own bodies.

The Last Practice of the Year, or The Party's Over!

The season's over, except for one last practice and the final game of the year. This one's all about having fun. As a coach, take a minute to reflect aloud with your team during a huddle about how far they've come. No matter what the wins and losses look like, touch on all the many improvements (refer back to those that you've recorded in your notebook) throughout the year. Thank your girls for their attention and energy and enthusiasm. Ask them to choose their four favorite drills. Run through them all and then follow these up with a no-holds-barred scrimmage. Make it a point to compliment each and every player by name. This will infect them with lasting energy and self-confidence, so that when they walk away from you and this season, they'll feel good about themselves and the sport of lacrosse. Isn't that what it's really all about?

Questions and Answers

Q. My recreation league doesn't provide trophies or awards. How can I reward my team?

A. You can often coordinate with parents to gather donations for team awards such as trophies, certificates, or team photos. Also, an end-of-season party is always a fun way to bring closure to and celebrate your season.

CHAPTER 9

Game Day

"Is this our bench?" "They look so much bigger than us!" "My mom brought oranges!" "My mouth guard just fell in the dirt!" "Can I play goalie?" "I feel so nervous!" "Do you have an extra uniform?" "Are they our refs?" "Stick check!" "Captains ready?"

Welcome to the Big Time, it's Game Day. The butterflies are out in force, threatening to blow away the confidence built up over a month of hard practicing. For many of your girls, this is their first taste of organized athletic competition. Otherwise unflappable kids warily eye the official as she checks to see if the pockets of their sticks are legal.

Take a deep breath and smile. The bottom line is that someone's going to win and someone's going to lose. You and your assistants, as well as the girls and their parents, must be prepared to accept either outcome with grace, good humor, and sportsmanship. Remind your players that you don't base success on the win or the loss, but on how well they demonstrate their understanding of what they've done in practice, the effort and hustle they put into the game, and the sportsmanship they display.

An attacker shoots—and scores!

Set a Good Example

On game day, one of the most important things coaches can do is set a good example for their players. How you behave on the sidelines will directly impact and influence your players, the fans, and your opponents. Your actions will speak volumes about your grasp of sportsmanship. Never more intently than today will your players be looking to you for guidance and encouragement. *How effectively you offer that guidance and encouragement is the true measure of your success as a coach—not the final score.*

Overview of the Game

Before the Game

You should arrive at least 45 minutes before game time. You've got things to do, people to meet.

Check the field to make sure it has been properly lined and set up.

Whistle your team to "Bring it in" to start them on a warm-up routine. Avoid talking about the game or your opponent right away. Keep the atmosphere fun and relaxed. Players will be nervous and excited, and you'll need to temper that energy. Check to make sure they all have water bottles, uniforms, sticks, and mouth guards. (It's a good idea to have spare uniforms and mouth guards in your equipment bag.) Have the girls jog a lap around the field; instruct designated players to lead stretching exercises and footwork drills. Ask your assistant coach or a parent to supervise partner passing, shuttles, and shooting drills.

Have the goalie warm up with a coach or conscientious parent. We strongly advise against pummeling a goalie in a pregame warm-up. More than anything else, she needs to take the field with her confidence intact. You want to make her feel like she's really seeing the ball. Do not allow her to be immediately fired on by her teammates. Shoot right at her stick at first, and then progress to shooting to areas where she can make a lot of saves in order to feel good about herself.

Get your team moving as the goalie continues to warm up. The field players should progress to doing one-on-ones, defensive footwork drills, and three-on-three play. The objective is to get them moving and thinking about their offensive and defensive concepts.

Meet and greet the officials, whether they're paid professionals, parent volunteers, or high school students. Shake hands and show them the respect they deserve. Be ready to hand the umpire a check (or cash) if payment is required.

Welcome the opposing team and introduce yourself to the coach while asking if there's anything they may need.

At this point the umpire will call for captains to explain the rules and ask if there are any questions. The umpire will flip a coin, and the winning captain will decide which goal cage her team will defend in the first half. Then the umpire will call a stick check for each team.

Stick checking is done by the umpire. (This is different from the stick checking discussed in chapter 5.) Here, the umpire is checking each player's stick to make sure the pocket is legal. To facilitate this, make sure all your players, including the goalie, form a single-file line, sticks in hand and mouth guards in mouths. (Remind your players that no jewelry or elaborate hair accessories

Girls tighten their pockets as an umpire calls "Stick check!"

are permitted during play.) A player with an illegal pocket will be asked to tighten it and must have it checked again before she is able to take the field.

Bring it in again when all the preliminaries are done. Announce to your team, with enthusiasm, the starting lineup. You might add, "For our players supporting the starting lineup, we plan on getting you into the game as soon as possible. We expect you to be paying attention to the game and cheering for your teammates on the field." End of discussion. Be direct and firm. Highlight two or three key concepts: "I want to see everyone hustle after ground balls, and I want to see the defense with their sticks up in the passing lanes." Conclude with a reminder to have fun and play hard. Give a "One, two, three . . ." to signal the start of a team cheer, after which the girls should sprint to their assigned positions for the center draw.

During the Game
From the Sidelines
At the 6- to 8-year-old level, most recreational rules allow for one coach from each side to be on the field during play. Limit your communication with a player to a particular play. The game moves too fast to analyze every action. Save the big-picture concept until the half or after the game. Be unobtrusive. It's a privilege to be out on the field, in the action, teaching and coaching your players; don't abuse it. When you're on the field, you'll need an assistant coach or parent volunteer supervising your substitutions and keeping order on the sidelines.

If you're coaching girls ages 8 and older, you'll have to stay on the sidelines during games. How you handle an injured player, a poor call by an official, a question about something that has occurred, a substantial goal advantage or deficit, or the excitement of a close game will define you as a coach. Think before you speak or act. Make sure all your comments are positive and constructive.

It's difficult to communicate with your players on the field during play. You might try hand signals or one-word reminders. For example, calling "Three!" may help them be aware of the 3-second rule, or "Good time!" might alert them that it's the right time to go to goal. Some coaches use color-coded cards to communicate with their players. Unless it's vital, save your more complicated and philosophical instructions or comments until players come off during substitutions.

Player Rotation
Think about how you plan to group the players. Will there be a first team and a second team based on ability? Or will you blend your players for team balance? It's your call, but be consistent. Lacrosse games are divided into two halves. Consider using time to determine player rotations. For instance, you might tell your team that midway through each half you'll substitute the attackers and defenders. Midfielders might need more frequent breaks, so

feel free to rotate them sooner. Younger players would probably do better with shorter rotations. You might ask one of your parents to alert you at 5-minute intervals. We've generally found that players on the sidelines are eagerly waiting their turns to go in. Encourage them to pay attention to the game and learn by watching.

Be aware that certain methods of substitution can send negative messages to members of your team and their parents, such as not playing certain players in "big games," playing some players only when you're winning by a dozen goals, or always starting the same players. Try rotating your starters based on which girls really hustled that week in practice, which girls attended practice regularly, or which girls were especially good listeners or helpers during practices. All players should sprint on and off the field during substitutions. Once they're off, they should get a drink and be ready to play again.

Time-Outs

The 2-minute time-out can be used to give your players a rest, stop the momentum of the opposing team, set up a special play on offense or defense, and get certain players into the game with particular assignments.

Each team is allowed one time-out per half. Time-outs can be called only after goals are scored. They can be called by a player on the field or by a coach. During time-outs, players need to hustle in to you and be ready to listen. Make your instructions and comments specific. Try not to throw too much information at your team in a short amount of time. Two minutes is plenty of time to make adjustments. You can refer back to things they've done during practices to explain your points. End the time-out with an energized team cheer before the players hustle back onto the field.

If the umpire calls an injury time-out, instruct your players to stay on the field where they stopped at the umpire's whistle, with their sticks on the ground. Coaches may not actively coach field players during these time-outs.

Halftime

Walk your players away from your bench area into a private space where you can talk freely without parent interaction or distraction. Give them a couple of minutes to talk and settle down and grab drinks and orange slices. While they're doing that, you might approach individuals to offer specific comments. Then it's time to address the group.

Focus on no more than a few specific points. For instance: "Girls, #4 has just scored the last three goals for the other team. Molly, I want you to tighten up on her on defense, and the rest of the defenders need to slide earlier on #4 for an effective double team."

Tell the team clearly and directly what they have to do. Don't ask them what they think they should do. In fact, we don't even like to ask them how they're feeling at this point, because if someone complains that she's tired, it puts that negative thought in everyone's mind. You don't want to in-

---

Minor Injuries? Think RICE

Bumps and bruises are a part of youth sports, and even though girls' lacrosse is among the safest activities, there is the risk, however slim, of catastrophic injury. Keep a cell phone on hand during games in case of emergency. For strains and sprains, the RICE method will help a minor soft-tissue injury heal faster.

- **Relative Rest.** Avoid activities that exacerbate the injury, but continue to move the injured area gently. Early gentle movement promotes healing.

- **Ice.** Apply ice to the affected area for 20 minutes and then leave it off for half an hour. *Note:* Don't use ice on a player who has circulatory problems.

- **Compression.** Compression creates a pressure gradient that reduces swelling and promotes healing. An elastic bandage provides a moderate amount of pressure that will help discourage swelling.

- **Elevation.** Elevation is especially effective when used in conjunction with compression. Elevation provides a pressure gradient. The higher the injured body part is raised, the more fluid is pulled away from the injury site via gravity. Elevate the injury as high above the heart as comfortable. Continue to elevate intermittently until swelling is gone.

---

stigate negativity at the half no matter what the score or game situation. Don't entertain questions from the team about the score. Let them know exactly what you want them to focus on in the next half. Period. Always end the half with an enthusiastic team cheer.

End of the Game

When the final whistle blows, regardless of the outcome of the game, here's the drill:

- Thank the officials for their efforts.
- Supervise your team and line up with them to shake hands with the opposing team. Spend an extra minute with the opposing coach to thank the team for the game and wish them luck in their season.
- Bring it In! Take a minute to discuss your team's performance, perhaps highlighting what you'll be working on during the next practice. Keep it short. Keep it positive. Finis.
- As with all your practices, make sure all the kids find a safe way home before you leave.

Congratulations, Coach! You've made it through your first game.

Questions and Answers

Q. What do I do about an official who seems worse than mediocre? She simply isn't controlling the game. I'm actually afraid for the safety of my players.

Pat Dillon on Umpires

The umpires are out there to help and teach. The problem is, the least experienced officials often officiate the youth games. There's a shortage of umpires, especially for youth games. It takes a special mind-set to be a youth umpire. They've got to be educators, not authoritative whistle-blowers.

There absolutely should be interaction between coaches and umpires, but *civilized interaction only.* The number-one job of an umpire is to keep the game safe.

My pet peeve? Coaches who, without having read the rules (much less attended any rules clinics for a more comprehensive understanding) scream and berate umpires. Read your rule book. Attend rules clinics. If you're going to confront an umpire, at least know your rules. Coaches have a right to dialogue with umpires; they can expect brief explanations during halftime breaks. But coaches need to be calm and open-minded during umpires' explanations. Umpires absolutely should be willing to take the time to explain themselves, when approached calmly and rationally. They shouldn't have the attitude of: "I'm the umpire and I'm always right!"

Pat Dillon, Rules Chair, Women's Division, US Lacrosse

A. The number-one job of an umpire is to keep the game safe. He or she has so many things to watch at once, especially considering that there's often only one umpire on the field (and he or she may be a volunteer) during youth games. The game has grown so much that we haven't been able to keep up with it in terms of quality coaches and umpires. Some umpires out there are doing it for the money: perhaps your game is their fifth in a row that day, and they're out of energy, physically, and their mental sharpness is waning. First, talk about your concerns to the umpire. If things don't improve, and you think the safety of your players is at all compromised, take your players off the field. (Courtesy Pat Dillon)

Q. What do I do about an unruly parent? She distracts my players. Even the umpire, who is young, seems intimidated by the negativity and yelling. Is it my responsibility or the umpire's to control this parent?

A. When you're setting up the season, appoint a parent to be field monitor. Make it a point to emphasize to all team members and parents that we're going to be the most sportsmanlike and positive group out there, bar none, by cheering for our kids—and the others, if they make a good play. And by all means, do not denigrate the official if she is less than perfect. It might even be worth your while to have everyone sign a contract agreeing to this. The field monitor (or coach) should bring them to games. If a parent gets out of hand, quietly hand her the signed contract and that should make the point, loud and clear. (Courtesy Pat Dillon)

CHAPTER 10

FUN-damental Drills Are Fun!

This chapter introduces the basic skills your players need to enjoy the game of women's lacrosse. This information, combined with the offensive and defensive drills in chapters 11 and 12, will help get you started.

Diagram key.

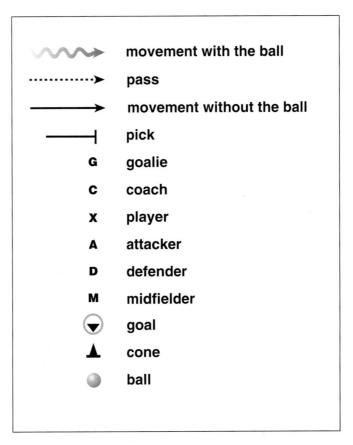

∿∿∿➤	movement with the ball
┄┄┄┄➤	pass
──────➤	movement without the ball
────┤	pick
G	goalie
C	coach
X	player
A	attacker
D	defender
M	midfielder
⊽	goal
▲	cone
●	ball

Warm-Up Drills

Fast Feet F1

Purpose: To increase foot speed and improve the ability to change direction quickly.

Number of Players: All
Equipment: None

```
        c              c →            ← c

 x    x    x  │  x → x → x →  │  ← x ← x ← x


 x    x    x  │  x → x → x →  │  ← x ← x ← x
```

1. Spread your players out into three lines facing you.
2. Have them bend their knees, as if in a seated position, to get into their defensive stance.
3. They should bend slightly at the waist and lean slightly forward.
4. Sticks are straight up and down, and their arms are comfortably away from their bodies.
5. On the whistle, players move from foot to foot as quickly as possible while keeping their head up and their body weight balanced. Execute "fast feet" for 10 to 15 seconds and then stop. Repeat several times to get your players warmed up.

This drill helps players increase their foot speed. Remind them that their sticks must remain straight up and down and their body weight must remain balanced.

Variations: Blow the whistle and point to your left (your players' right). While still facing you, players must move in that direction, still maintaining their fast feet by taking small, quick, balanced steps. Now blow the whistle and point to the right (your players' left). They must change direction quickly (while still facing forward) and move to their left while maintaining their fast feet by taking small, quick, balanced steps. Do this for 30 seconds and then give the team a chance to shake their legs out. Repeat three times.

Flag Tag F2

Purpose: To teach the fundamentals of space and movement, and to build agility and quickness.	**Number of Players:** 9 (8 attackers, 1 defender) **Equipment:** 4 cones, 8 practice jerseys

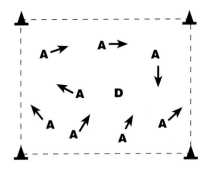

1. Place four cones in a 30-by-30-yard grid.
2. Nine players (without sticks) play at one time.
3. The eight attackers use their practice jersey as a flag, which they tuck into their shorts leaving half of it exposed.
4. The object is for the defender to tag an attacker by grabbing her flag and pulling it out of her shorts.
5. The attackers must move around the grid and try to avoid being tagged by using quick change-of-direction moves and anticipating where the defender is going.
6. If tagged, the attacker gives her jersey to the defender, and then she becomes the defender. The new defender can't catch the original defender but must attempt to tag other players. Modify the drill by adding additional defenders, one at a time.

The game of tag is basic to the concept of understanding open and closed spaces. Offensive players need to move to open spaces by scanning the field and making good decisions about where to move and how to get there without coming into contact with others.

Grab-a-Ball Tag F3

Purpose: To develop change of speed and direction and movement into open space.	**Number of Players:** 9 (8 attackers, 1 defender) **Equipment:** 4 cones, 4 balls

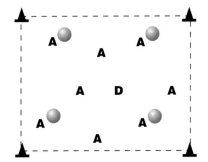

1. Set up four cones in a 20-by-20-yard grid.
2. Designate one player to be a defender inside the square.
3. Scatter the eight attackers inside the square and give four of them a ball to hold in their hand (no sticks).
4. The defender must tag a player with a ball. Once she does, the tagged player becomes the defender, and the original defender joins the offensive players.

5. The players with a ball can pass the ball to another attacker who doesn't have a ball. If a player with a ball chooses to pass the ball to a player without one, the player without the ball has to take it and be aware of where the defender is.

Stick-Work Drills

Stick-work tricks are designed to help your players become comfortable with handling their stick. They are fun, creative ways to enhance your players' ability to handle the ball at all levels. Stick-work tricks encourage your players to have soft hands and a relaxed upper body when cradling, throwing, and catching. They inspire your players to handle their stick in ways they never thought possible. Be creative! Think outside the box! Practice really does make perfect, and stick-work tricks really do improve stick work. These stick-work tricks are described for a right-handed player, yet each one should be done with both the right and left hand.

Toss and Catch F4

Purpose: To develop the ability to cradle and handle the stick creatively with both hands.	**Number of Players:** All **Equipment:** 1 ball per player

1. Each player starts with the ball in the pocket and with the stick out in front of her body, parallel to the ground.
2. The player's top hand should be at least one-third of the way down the stick, and her bottom hand should be at the bottom of the stick for control.
3. With her knees bent and her body in a balanced position, the player tosses the ball into the air, rotates the stick with her fingertips and wrists, and catches the ball on the back of the pocket of her stick. Tell players to give with the catch as if they were catching an egg.
4. The player continues to toss the ball from the back of the stick into the air, rotate the stick with her fingertips and wrists, and catch the ball (she alternates catching it front and back). The bottom hand should do most of the work; the top hand is the guide.
5. Players start with their stick in their dominant hand, toss and catch 10 times, and then repeat with the nondominant hand.

This trick improves hand-eye coordination and encourages soft hands.

Bounce off the Shaft F5

Stick trick: popping the ball off the stick shaft.

Purpose: To develop the ability to cradle and handle the stick creatively with both hands.	**Number of Players:** All **Equipment:** 1 ball per player

1. Each player starts with the ball in the stick, holding it in the right hand.
2. Her hand is about 2 inches from the head of the stick for control.
3. The player tosses the ball into the air, brings the stick parallel to the ground with the stick head by her right ear, and bounces the ball off the stick shaft.
4. The player pops the ball straight up off the stick shaft and catches it.
5. The player repeats the bounce and catch 10 times and then switches to the left hand.

Remind players to bounce the ball straight up, not out away from their body, to make it easier to catch.

Bounce off the Sidewall F6

Popping the ball off the sidewall.

Purpose: To develop the ability to cradle and handle the stick creatively with both hands.	**Number of Players:** All **Equipment:** 1 ball per player

1. Each player starts with the ball in the stick.
2. The player has both hands on the stick. The top hand is about one-third of the way down the stick, and the bottom hand is at the bottom of the stick for control.
3. With her knees bent and her body in a balanced position, the player holds the stick out in front of her body, parallel to the ground.
4. The player tosses the ball into the air, rotates the stick with her fingertips and wrists, and bounces the ball off the sidewall of the stick head.
5. The player pops the ball straight up off the sidewall and catches it in the stick.

6. The player repeats 10 times and then switches to the nondominant hand.

    Variation: Have players try bouncing the ball on the sidewall as many times as possible before catching it.

Toss and Catch, Front and Back   F7

Purpose: To develop the ability to cradle and handle the stick creatively with both hands.	**Number of Players:** All
	Equipment: 1 ball per player

Catching the ball behind the back.

1. Each player starts with the ball in the stick, holding it in her right hand. Her right hand should be placed about one-third of the way down the stick shaft.
2. With her knees bent and her body in a balanced position, the player positions the stick at the right hip, parallel to the ground.
3. The player tosses the ball across her body to the left side and catches it behind her back.
4. After the toss, the player drops the stick head down, behind her right hip so that the stick is perpendicular to the ground, and then uses her wrist to bring the stick back up behind her back to catch the ball on her left side.
5. From behind the back, the player uses a flip of the wrist to toss the ball in front of her body and catch it.
6. The player repeats the movement 10 times and then switches to the left hand.

    When players move the stick from in front of the body to behind the back, and vice versa, they should remember to drop the head of the stick down and perpendicular to the ground and then bring it back up again.

Toss and Catch between the Legs F8

Purpose: To develop the ability to cradle and handle the stick creatively with both hands.

Number of Players: All
Equipment: 1 ball per player

Stick trick: catching the ball between the legs.

1. Each player starts with the ball in the stick, holding it in the right hand. Her right hand should be placed about one-third of the way down the stick shaft.
2. With her knees bent and her body in a balanced position, the player positions the stick at the right hip, parallel to the ground.
3. The player tosses the ball across the body to the left side and catches it behind her back.
4. After the toss, the player drops the stick head down, behind her right hip so that the stick is perpendicular to the ground, and then uses her wrist to bring the stick back up behind her back to catch the ball on her left side.
5. From behind her back, the player uses a flip of the wrist to toss the ball in front of her body.
6. Instead of catching the ball in front of the body, the player brings the stick up between her legs and catches the ball between her legs.
7. The player uses a flip of her wrist to toss the ball into the air and catch it behind her back again.
8. The player repeats the movement 10 times and then switches the stick to her left hand.

When players are moving the stick from behind their back to between their legs, and vice versa, they should remember to drop the head of the stick down and perpendicular to the ground and then bring it back up again.

Cradle and Twirl F9

Purpose: To improve stick handling and cradling ability with both hands.

Number of Players: All
Equipment: 1 ball per player

1. Each player cradles the ball on the right side of her head, from the ear to the nose (see Cradling on pages 41–43) and with the right hand placed about one-third of the way down the stick.
2. After a few cradles, when the stick is back by her ear, the player uses her fingertips to twirl the stick in a circular motion away from her head.
3. The player keeps her bottom hand in by her body while her top hand and arm extend slightly out from her body.
4. As the stick is twirled back into the regular cradle position, the ear-to-nose cradle begins again.
5. The player should remember to make a circle with the stick as it is twirled away from the head and then back to the ear. The ball remains on the *inside* of the circle. The player repeats the movement 10 times and then switches the stick to the left side of her head.

Cradle and Extended Twirl F10

Purpose: To improve stick handling and cradling ability with both hands.

Number of Players: All
Equipment: 1 ball per player

1. Each player cradles the ball on the right side of her head, from the ear to the nose and with the right hand placed about one-third of the way down the stick.
2. After a few cradles, when the stick is back by the ear, the player uses her fingertips to twirl the stick in a circular motion away from her head.
3. The player keeps her bottom hand in by the body, but she steps with the left foot and extends the top hand and arm out from and *across* the body, really exaggerating the twirl.
4. As the stick is twirled back into the regular cradle position, the player brings her left foot back so the ear-to-nose cradle can begin again.
5. The player should make an exaggerated circle with the stick as it is twirled away from her head, really reach with her top hand and arm, and then bring her stick back to her ear. Again, the ball remains on the inside of the circle. The player repeats the movement 10 times and then switches the stick to the left side of her head.

This drill is a variation of the Cradle and Twirl.

Wall Ball Routine **F11**

> **Purpose:** To improve stick handling, cradling, throwing, and catching with both hands.
>
> **Number of Players:** All
> **Equipment:** 1 wall, 1 ball per player

1. Position players 6 to 8 feet away from a wall. Their top hand should be placed at least one-third of the way down the stick and their bottom hand should be out in front of the body.
2. With the stick in her right hand and her right hand up, each player throws the ball, bounces it off the wall, and catches it right-handed. She repeats 10 times and does a dip dodge (see pages 53–54) to the left hand.
3. With the stick in her left hand and her left hand up, the player throws and catches the ball left-handed. She repeats 10 times and does a dip dodge to the right hand.
4. With her right hand up, the player throws right-handed, catches right-handed, and does an extended twirl reaching to the left and then to the right. She repeats 10 times and does a dip dodge to the left hand.
5. With her left hand up, the player throws left-handed, catches left-handed, and does an extended twirl reaching to the right and then to the left. She repeats 10 times and does a dip dodge to the right hand.
6. With her right hand up, cradling on her right side, the player twirls her stick away from her head, throws right-handed, and catches the ball on the weak side. She should remember to flip her stick over, use soft hands so she can give with the catch, and push out her bottom hand. She repeats 10 times and then passes her stick through her legs to the left hand.
7. With her left hand up, cradling on her left side, the player twirls her stick away from her head, throws left-handed, and catches the ball on the weak side. She should remember to flip her stick over, use soft hands so she can give with the catch, and push out her bottom hand. She repeats 10 times and then passes her stick through her legs to her right hand.
8. With her right hand up, the player twirls away from her head twice, throws right-handed, catches right-handed, switches quickly to her left, twirls away from her head twice, throws left-handed, catches left-handed, and switches quickly to her right into her passing position. She repeats the series 10 times.
9. With her right hand up, the player drops her stick to her right hip, twirls once, passes sidearm, catches right, and does a dip dodge to her left. She drops her stick to her left hip, twirls once, passes sidearm, catches left, and does a dip dodge to her right. She repeats the series 10 times.

10. With her right hand up, the player tosses the ball high on the wall so she really has to reach for it on the catch. She catches five balls with two hands on the stick (slid down to the bottom to get a good extension) and five balls with one hand on the stick (slid almost to the bottom of the stick so she still has some control). She should remember to pull the stick in quickly to her head on the catch and begin cradling.

11. With her left hand up, the player tosses the ball high on the wall so she really has to reach for it on the catch. She catches five balls with two hands on the stick (slid down to the bottom to get a good extension) and five balls with one hand on the stick (slid almost to the bottom of the stick so she still has some control). She should remember to pull the stick in quickly to her head on the catch and begin cradling.

Players should use soft hands—handling the stick with their fingertips and letting it rest lightly in the palm of their top hand. Their shoulders should be relaxed, they should turn slightly with every catch, and they should have more of a rotation on each throw. Their stance should be with feet shoulder-width apart and with one foot slightly in front of the other (left foot in front when throwing right-handed, right foot in front when throwing left-handed). When catching, players should ask for the ball in front on the side of the head and give back softly (catching it behind the ear). Their shoulders should turn when they give back with the ball to protect the stick. When throwing, the bottom hand should be out in front; they should use a push (with the top hand) and a pull (with the bottom hand) motion and re-member to snap the wrist. The shoulders should rotate on the throw to give power and accuracy, and they should follow through across the body.

Passing and Catching Drills

Partner Passing F12

Purpose: To improve cradling, stick work, passing, and catching.	Number of Players: 12, in pairs Equipment: 1 ball

1. Position partners in two lines about 7 yards apart facing each other.
2. Partners pass the ball back and forth, starting with two hands on the stick for the catch and only the right hand on the stick for the pass.
3. Partners pass with two hands on the stick for the catch and only the left hand on the stick for the pass.
4. Partners pass with two hands on the stick, first a right-handed pass and catch and then left-handed.
5. Partners pass with quick sticks by receiving the ball and passing it back all in one motion.
6. Partners pass with quick sticks, using the back of the stick.
7. Partners make long passes to one another. They keep backing up to see how far apart they can be and still throw and catch without dropping the ball. Emphasize to players that they should rotate their hips and shoulders, step into the pass, and snap their wrist to get greater distance on the ball.
8. Partners pass using flip passes (see pages 48–49).
9. Partners pass using behind-the-back passes (see page 49).
10. Partners pass using reverse-stick passes (see page 50).
11. Partners catch and pass between their legs.
12. Partners pass with high lob passes (see pages 49–50), catching first with two hands and then with one hand.
13. Drill continues for 10 to 12 minutes.

Partner passing is a terrific way to give your players lots of touches on the ball. Key points to emphasize are keeping their feet moving on the pass and catch, with one foot in front of the other; asking for the ball to the side of their head; and rotating their shoulders on the pass and catch.

Triples F13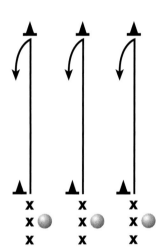

Purpose: To improve cradling, passing, catching, and changing direction (pivoting).	Number of Players: 9, in groups of three Equipment: 2 cones per group, 1 ball per group

1. Have players get into groups of three and line up behind a cone for each group.
2. Place another cone 10 yards away from the first cone. The second player in each line has a ball.
3. The first player in line cuts to the farther cone, pivots, and turns back toward the player with the ball, asking for the ball on her right-hand side.
4. The player with the ball passes it as soon as she sees her teammate pivot.
5. After she passes the ball, she cuts to the far cone.
6. Drill continues for 2 to 3 minutes.

   Variations: Throw right, catch right; throw left, catch left; throw right, catch left; throw left, catch right; flip pass right, flip pass left; reverse-stick pass right, reverse-stick pass left; ground balls.

FUN-DAMENTAL DRILLS

FUN-DAMENTAL DRILLS

Work-the-Point Passing F14

Purpose: To teach the fundamentals of passing and catching.	**Number of Players:** All, in groups of four
	Equipment: 3 balls per group

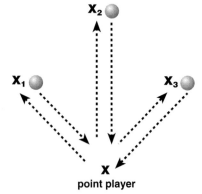

1. Have players get into groups of four. Each group forms an 8-by-8-yard diamond.
2. Three players in each group have balls, and one player, the point player, does not.
3. The players with balls take turns passing to the open (point) player, one after another.
4. The open player must keep her feet moving and shift her position so she can catch and pass the ball back accurately to the player who passed her the ball.
5. Drill continues for about 10 minutes.

Variations: Catch and pass all right-handed, all left-handed; catch left, throw right; catch right, throw left; flip pass; quick sticks (players may need to move in a little closer).

Square Passing F15

Purpose: To develop quick, accurate passing and catching skills.	**Number of Players:** All, in groups of four
	Equipment: 4 cones per group, 1 ball per group

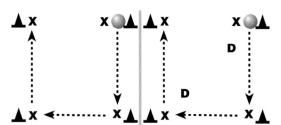

1. Have players get into groups of four. Each group forms a 10-by-10-yard square. Each player stands by a cone.
2. Players pass the ball around the outside of the square (no diagonal passes) as quickly as possible.
3. On the whistle, players must pass the ball in the opposite direction.
4. Encourage players to keep their stick on the outside of the square when passing and catching to simulate keeping the stick away from defenders inside the square.
5. Drill continues for about 10 minutes.

Variations: Ask the players to twirl their stick away from their head before they pass. Or ask players to fake before they pass. Add a defender or two inside the square to put pressure on the pass and catch (right diagram).

Blob Passing F16

Purpose: To develop the ability to move the ball quickly to an open player and to move without the ball.	**Number of Players:** All **Equipment:** Balls for half the team

1. All players are inside the 12-meter fan.
2. Half of the players have a ball, and the other half do not.
3. On the whistle the players must begin moving around the 12-meter fan.
4. The players with a ball must pass to an open player and then cut to receive a ball from someone else.
5. Players must keep their head up to pass or receive and must be aware of what is going on around them.
6. Drill continues for about 10 minutes.

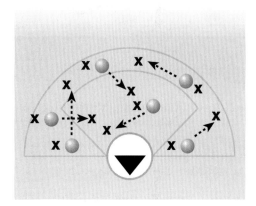

Pass-Back Weave F17

Purpose: To develop the ability to throw and catch long passes across the field.	**Number of Players:** All, in groups of three
	Equipment: 1 ball per group

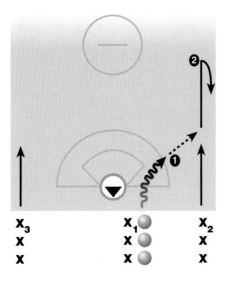

1. Have players form three lines at the end line with the ball in the middle line.
2. The first players in each line (group 1) begin to move down the field.
3. The first ball carrier (X1) passes to the first player in either of the outside lines. This player (X2) catches the ball and immediately runs straight upfield along the sideline while X1 trails her by about 15 to 20 yards.
4. X2 runs upfield for about 20 to 25 yards, breaks her stride, pivots toward the outside of the field (to avoid any defenders), leads with her stick, and quickly passes the ball back to her trailing teammate, X1.
5. Once X2 passes back, she sprints toward the player (X3) on the opposite side of the field.
6. X1 receives the ball from X2 at least 15 to 20 yards behind the passer (X2) and immediately sets her feet and passes the ball across the field to the player in the opposite line (X3), who has remained even with the trailing player (X2).
7. The player in the opposite line (X3) receives the ball and sprints upfield as her trail pass player (X2) gets into position and the drill repeats itself.
8. When the first group reaches the 50-yard line, the next group starts off.
9. Drill continues until each group has gone to the opposite end line and back twice.

The pass-back weave encourages the development of long passes across the width of the field that allow teams to "swing the ball" to the opposite side of the field and get out of defensive pressure, or change their point of attack.

Triangle Passing F18

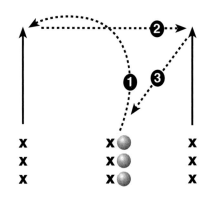

Purpose: To improve the ability to lob pass, lateral pass, and pick up a ground ball on the move.	Number of Players: All, in groups of three
	Equipment: 1 ball per group

1. Have players form three lines at the end line with the ball in the middle line.
2. The first players in each line (group 1) begin to jog down the field in a triangle formation.
3. The middle player chooses to pass an over-the-shoulder pass (or lob pass—see pages 49–50) to one of the players on either side of her.
4. That player catches the ball and passes it laterally across the field to the other outside player.
5. The third player catches the ball and rolls a ground ball back to the middle player, who picks it up and then throws a lob pass to either side. Have players catch and pass laterally and catch and roll ground balls until they reach the opposite end line.
6. Drill continues until each group has gone to the opposite end line and back twice.

   Variation: Have players twirl their stick before releasing the ball.

Three in One F19

Purpose: To develop passing, catching, pivoting, and picking up ground balls.	Number of Players: 4 Equipment: 3 cones, 1 ball

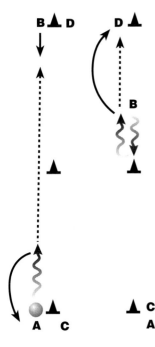

1. Place three cones about 10 yards apart on the field in a straight line.
2. There are two players at each outside cone (players A and C and players B and D).
3. Player A begins with the ball, passes to player B, and moves behind player C (left diagram).
4. Player B catches the pass, pivots at the middle cone, rolls a ground ball to player D, and moves behind player D (right diagram).
5. Player D picks up the ground ball, passes to player C, and moves behind player B.
6. Player C catches the ball, pivots at the cone, rolls a ground ball to player A, and moves behind A.
7. Drill continues for 2 to 3 minutes.

Ground Ball Drills

Ground Ball Tag F20

Purpose: To improve the ability to pick up a ground ball under pressure.	Number of Players: 9 (8 attackers, 1 defender) Equipment: 4 cones, 2 balls

1. Set up a 30-by-30-yard grid with four cones.
2. One player without a stick is the defender who is "it."
3. The remaining eight players have sticks and are the offense; two of the eight players have a ball.
4. On the whistle, the offensive players have to roll ground balls to each other while cutting inside the grid. The defender tries to tag an offensive

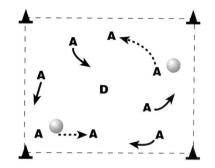

player who has a ball before the offensive player can roll it to a teammate, or as the teammate picks up the ground ball.

5. Once someone is tagged while holding the ball, she becomes the defender, and the other player takes her place with the offense.

6. Drill continues for 2 to 3 minutes.

Variations: Add three balls to the drill. Require the offense to twirl their stick before they can roll the ground ball. Add another defender.

Competitive Ground Balls F21

Purpose: To develop the ability to pick up a ground ball under pressure and beat a double team.	**Number of Players:** All (including goalie)
	Equipment: 1 goal, 10 balls

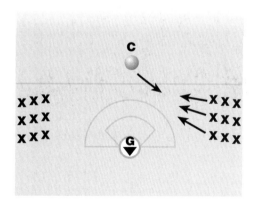

1. Split the team in half.

2. Position players in three lines on either side of the goal cage about 10 yards from the corners of the 8-meter arc.

3. The coach or an assistant stands at the 25-yard line with the balls.

4. One group of three players goes at a time. The coach rolls a ball toward a group of three, and the players work individually to pick up the ball.

5. Once a player has picked up the ground ball, she looks to go to the cage. The other two players become defenders and try to double-team (see pages 80–81) the ball carrier.

6. In this drill, players should attack the ground ball with speed while trying to cut the other players off.

7. Once a player picks up the ground ball, she must protect it from the defenders and look to get a shot off.

8. Drill continues for 5 to 7 minutes.

Ground Ball Blob Passing F22

Purpose: To teach the fundamentals of running through a ground ball pickup and moving without the ball.	**Number of Players:** 12 **Equipment:** 6 balls

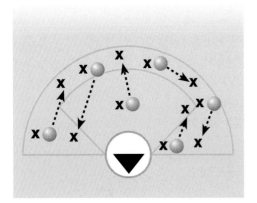

1. All players are inside the 12-meter fan.
2. Half of the players have a ball, and the other half do not.
3. On the whistle the players must begin moving around the 12-meter fan.
4. The players with a ball must roll a ground ball to an open player and then cut to receive a ground ball from someone else.
5. Players must keep their head up to pass or receive and must be aware of what is going on around them.
6. Drill continues for 3 to 5 minutes.

Dodging Drills

It's always good to break down dodges and have your players do them in pairs first so they know exactly what you are looking for as they execute the dodge.

Partner Dodging F23

Purpose: To learn the fundamental techniques of dodging.	**Number of Players:** All, in pairs **Equipment:** 1 ball per pair

1. Each player teams up with a partner, and the partners scatter around the playing field.
2. One partner becomes a stationary defender, and the other partner tries to get the ball past the defender by executing a dodge, such as the face dodge, dip dodge, sword dodge, roll dodge, and change-of-hands dodge (see pages 51–56).
3. Players repeat each dodge several times and then switch roles.
4. The coach moves among the partners, observing their technique.
5. Drill continues for 5 minutes.

FUN-DAMENTAL DRILLS

Pass and Dodge in Fours F24

Purpose: To develop dodging techniques under moderate pressure.

Number of Players: 4
Equipment: 2 cones, 1 ball

1. Place two cones 20 yards apart.
2. Specify which dodge you are working on.
3. There are two players behind each cone. Player A, who has the ball, passes to player B at the other cone, and runs to the midpoint between the two cones.
4. Player B catches the ball, attacks the midpoint between the two cones, and executes a dodge to get past player A. Player A continues to the opposite cone.
5. Player B passes to player C and becomes the defender in the middle of the cones.
6. Player C catches the ball, attacks the middle of the cones, and executes a dodge to get past player B. Player B continues to the opposite cone.
7. Player C passes to player D and becomes the defender in the middle of the cones.
8. Drill continues for 5 minutes.

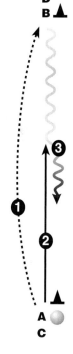

Five-on-Five Dodging Box F25

Purpose: To develop the fundamental techniques of dodging.

Number of Players: 10 (5 attackers, 5 defenders)
Equipment: 4 cones, 5 balls

1. Create a 20-by-20-yard grid with four cones.
2. Space five defenders evenly throughout the box. These players are stationary obstacles for the attackers, or dodgers.
3. Space five attackers in the grid, each with a ball.
4. Call out the dodge you want your attackers to execute. Play begins on your whistle.
5. Each attacker attacks a defender and executes the dodge that you've specified. They must then change direction and dodge another defender. This continues for 1 minute. Then blow your whistle and have the players switch roles.
6. Drill continues for 4 to 6 minutes.

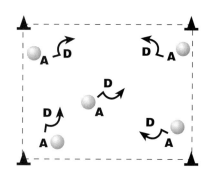

Box Dodging F26

Purpose: To develop dodging techniques in limited space and under moderate pressure.	**Number of Players:** 2 (1 attacker, 1 defender) **Equipment:** 4 cones, 1 ball

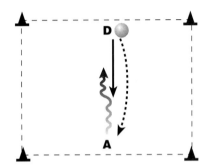

1. Place four cones in a 10-by-10-yard grid.
2. Two players, an attacker and a defender, stand on opposite sides of the grid, facing each other.
3. The defender starts with the ball and passes it to the attacker.
4. The attacker tries to dodge past the defender and make it across the imaginary line between the two cones on the defender's side of the box.
5. Play continues until the attacker makes it over the line, the defender steals the ball, or the defender forces the attacker outside the box on either side.
6. Award a point to the attacker if she makes it over the line and a point to the defender if she steals the ball or forces the attack player outside of the box. The game continues until one player reaches 5 points. Then players switch roles.

Shooting Drills

Triple Shot F27

Purpose: To develop the shooting technique for outside shots and shots close to the crease.	**Number of Players:** 10 (9 field players, 1 goalie) **Equipment:** 1 goal, 1 bucket of balls

1. Have three players line up at the 15-yard line with balls in the middle of the field (A).
2. Have three players line up about 5 yards outside the point of the 8-meter arc (in the 6-spot) with balls (B).
3. Have three players line up behind the crease (in the 1-spot) with balls (C).
4. The drill starts with the first player in group A taking an outside shot from the 12-meter fan.

5. She then settles her feet and receives a pass from the first player in group B and shoots from right inside the 8-meter arc.

6. The player from group A then cuts to the top of the 8-meter arc, pivots, and catches a feed from the first player in group C. She finishes with a one-on-one with the goalie in tight. Players rotate counterclockwise.

7. Drill continues for 10 minutes.

To include more players, set up two goal cages.

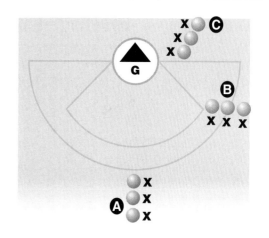

Star Shooting F28

Purpose: To develop passing, catching, and shooting ability.	**Number of Players:** 11 (10 field players, 1 goalie) **Equipment:** 1 goal, 5 cones, 1 bucket of balls

1. Set up five cones around the goal with two players behind each cone.

2. The rule of the drill: Always pass to the player two lines to the right. Balls start with player Xa. Player Xa passes to player Xc and replaces (runs) behind cone C.

3. Player Xc passes to player Xe and replaces behind cone E.

4. Player Xe passes to player Xb and replaces behind cone B.

5. Player Xb passes to player Xd and replaces behind cone D.

6. Player Xd catches the ball and goes down the pipes for a shot on goal.

7. Action repeats with the second group of players.

8. Drill continues for 10 to 12 minutes.

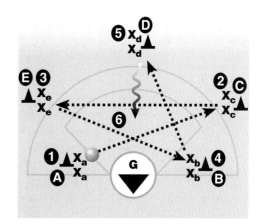

Variation: After Xb passes to Xd, Xb becomes the defender, and it's a one-on-one to goal with Xb versus Xd.

FUN-DAMENTAL DRILLS

Shooting Shuttle F29

Purpose: To develop the technique of passing and releasing a quick shot.

Number of Players: 11 (10 field players, 1 goalie)
Equipment: 1 goal, 1 bucket of balls

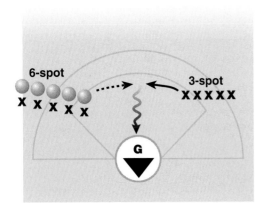

1. Have a line of five players in the 6-spot and a line of five players in the 3-spot at the top of the 8-meter arc.
2. Players in the 6-spot have balls. The first player in the 6-spot feeds the first player in the 3-spot, who catches and shoots on goal, making sure to step down the pipes on her shot.
3. Each player goes to the end of the opposite line, and the next player in the 6-spot feeds the next player in the 3-spot, who catches and shoots on goal. Action repeats—the drill continues for 7 to 10 minutes.

Lead with Your Head F30

Purpose: To develop the ability to look at the cage before shooting to increase accuracy.

Number of Players: 4 (3 attackers, 1 goalie)
Equipment: 1 goal, 1 bucket of balls

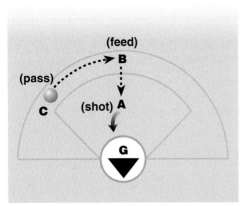

1. Player A stands about 5 to 7 yards in front of the goal, with her back to the goal cage.
2. Player B stands about 5 yards away from player A.
3. Player C has the bucket of balls and stands off to either side of player B.
4. Player A is the shooter. Tell her where you want her to shoot (top left corner, top right corner, middle left, middle right, bottom left corner, or bottom right corner).
5. Player C passes the ball to player B, who catches and feeds player A.
6. Player A catches, leads with her head, pivots on both feet, rotates her shoulders and hips, and snaps her wrist on the shot to goal. She then rotates back to receive another feed. The drill is

continuous, with players rotating positions after 5 or 10 balls have been played.

7. The goalie does her best to save the ball and then quickly resets for the next shot.

8. Repeat until each player has rotated through each position twice.

This shooting drill reinforces the concept of leading with the head before shooting. Emphasize that players need to see where they want to shoot and place the ball as opposed to just throwing it at the goal. Encourage your shooters to turn their head first, then their shoulders and hips on the shot. Have them see the net and shoot at it, rather than seeing the goalie. If possible, do this drill at two goal cages or more.

Four Corners with a Shot F31

Purpose: To develop the ability to cut off a pick, catch, and shoot.	Number of Players: 9 (8 field players, 1 goalie) Equipment: 1 goal, 1 bucket of balls

1. Set up four lines, with two players in each line, in a square around the goal cage. The goalie is in the cage.

2. The first player from group A (Xa) starts with the ball. Player Xa passes to player Xb and then drifts into the middle of the 8-meter arc, preparing to set a pick.

3. Player Xb passes to player Xc and stays high, waiting for the pick.

4. Player Xc passes to player Xd while player Xa sets a pick for player Xb.

5. As player Xd rolls around the crease, player Xb cuts off the pick, and player Xd feeds the ball to player Xb.

6. When player Xb cuts off the pick and takes a shot on goal, player Xa flashes to the opposite side, looking for a feed or rebound.

7. Drill continues for 10 to 12 minutes.

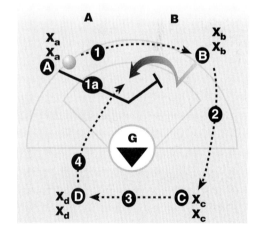

This drill works on moving the ball in settled offense and feeding a cutter off a pick.

CHAPTER 11

Offensive Drills

This chapter provides drills that break down the components of team offense into small parts and progresses to drills that support the entire team executing successfully on offense.

Breaking down your offensive concepts into smaller components allows your players to understand the basics of team offense and build from there. (Always remember to have enough practice jerseys to distinguish the offensive players from the defensive players!) A number of these drills set up the concepts being taught, meaning the four-on-three starts out of a stationary position. As the skill level of your team increases, we encourage you to make the offensive and defensive combination drills continuous by adding another goal cage and making the attackers play defense and the defenders play offense. Remember, we are developing complete players!

Continuous One-on-One to Goal 01

Purpose: To develop the courage to challenge a defender in a one-on-one situation.	**Number of Players:** 12 (10 field players, 2 goalies) **Equipment:** 2 goals, 1 bucket of balls

1. Set up two goals facing each other about 25 yards apart.
2. Half of the players stand about 10 yards to the right of goal 1, and half stand about 10 yards to the right of goal 2.
3. Have balls in each line.
4. Player A1 begins by attacking goal 2.
5. Player B1 becomes the defender.
6. Player A1 goes toward the goal until a shot, save, turnover, or goal occurs.

7. If a shot, save, or goal occurs, A1 becomes the defender, and B1 begins her attack on goal 1.
8. If the original play results in a turnover, B1 goes toward goal 1, and A1 now defends.
9. Drill continues for 7 to 10 minutes.

Whenever an attacker receives the ball in settled offense, she should look to challenge her defender and put pressure on the defense as a unit. Attackers should be encouraged to go down the pipes when challenging one-on-one to give themselves the best angle for shooting. This drill emphasizes the role of the attacker with the ball to penetrate with a dodge and a shot to put pressure on the defense. Encourage attackers to get a shot off quickly as opposed to making lots of moves in the 8-meter arc.

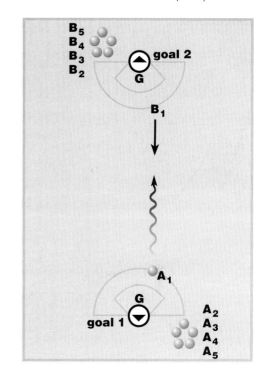

Offensive Three-on-Two to Goal 02

Purpose: To recognize and take advantage of being a player up offensively.	**Number of Players:** 6 (5 field players, 1 goalie) **Equipment:** 1 goal, 1 practice jersey per player, 1 bucket of balls

1. One attacker stands in line at the 40-yard line with balls.
2. Two attackers and two defenders stand at the top of the 12-meter fan.
3. Play starts with the ball carrier bringing the ball down from the 40-yard line toward the goal (left diagram). Her objective is to go straight to the goal at top speed to maintain the player advantage. She must decide before reaching the 12-meter fan whether to pass or shoot.
4. The two attackers close to the goal must get to either side of the crease while seeing the ball. They don't want to cut to

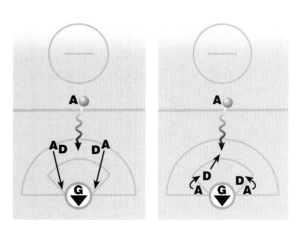

the player with the ball because they'll bring their defender to her. They want to give the ball carrier as much space as possible to attack the goal.

5. As the defender slides to the ball, the attacker whose defender left her must curl into the passing lane in good position to catch and shoot.

6. The opposite attacker should mirror her in an open passing lane and be ready to retrieve the rebound or missed shot or be prepared to receive the second pass and shoot (right diagram).

7. The ball carrier must read the defender who's not sliding to the ball; she dictates which attacker is open.

8. Drill continues until each player has had several turns at each position, about 10 to 12 minutes.

This drill sets up the three-on-two to goal so the offense can see how effective spacing and curling into passing lanes can take advantage of a defense that is a player down. The attackers should put themselves in positions to see each other (passing lanes) and avoid getting "lost" behind defenders. The two low attackers near the goal must get to the goal line extended, next to the crease, to give the ball carrier space to attack the cage. In a player-up situation the low attackers want to avoid cutting up to the ball carrier as they will bring their defense to her and take away the player-up advantage. They also want to avoid going behind the goal as the ball is coming down; this also will take away the player-up advantage. However, remind the low attackers to hustle after the missed shot as it goes behind the goal!

Variation: As your players' level of understanding improves, make this drill continuous by adding another goal cage (about 30 yards apart), and make the attackers play defense and the defenders play offense in a continuous three-on-two situation.

Offensive Four-on-Three to Goal 03

Purpose: To maintain field balance and spacing to create scoring opportunities in a four-on-three situation.	Number of Players: 8 (4 attackers, 3 defenders, 1 goalie) Equipment: 1 goal, 1 practice jersey per player, 10 balls

1. Set up two attackers (one with a ball) at the 30-yard line.

2. A defender stands in between the two attackers at the 15-yard line.

3. Two attackers and two defenders begin at the top of the 12-meter fan.

4. The play starts with one of the attackers at the 30-yard line bringing the ball downfield.

5. The two attackers in the 12-meter must get to the crease while seeing the ball. This forces their defenders to go with them and creates space for the ball carrier. If a defender does not go with a low attacker, the ball carrier can pass the ball to her open teammate over the defender's stick.

6. The four attackers want to stay in a box formation to try to stretch the defense as much as possible. The ball carrier, staying on her original side, carries the ball until she is picked up (meaning a defender has slid to play her). Once picked up, she moves the ball to the open player.

7. If the defense doesn't slide, the player should shoot. The other attackers should be ready to back up the shot.

8. The ball carrier should force defensive players to commit to her and should move the ball as the defense moves.

9. The ball carrier must read the diagonal defender—she dictates which attacker is open.

10. Drill continues until each player has had a turn in each position.

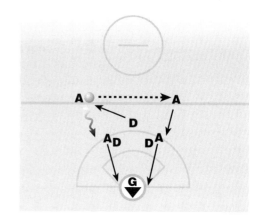

Four-on-three situations happen often in girls' lacrosse, especially after a foul when a defender gets put behind the attacker who was fouled. This drill will help your players recognize the four-on-three and maintain the spacing necessary to capitalize on it. Notice that the attackers stay in a box formation as the ball moves toward the cage. The player with the ball should attack the goal from her side, looking to draw the top defender and pass, or she should shoot if the defender doesn't slide in time. As in the three-on-two, the low attackers want to get to the goal line extended to give the ball carrier space to attack the goal cage and make the slide longer for the defense.

Variation: As your players' level of understanding improves, make this drill continuous by adding another goal cage (about 30 yards apart) and make the attackers play defense and the defenders play offense in a continuous four-on-three situation.

Offensive Five-on-Four to Goal 04

Purpose: To develop attacking techniques and concepts to use when there is an extra player.	**Number of Players:** 10 (5 attackers, 4 defenders, 1 goalie) **Equipment:** 1 goal, 1 practice jersey per player, 10 balls

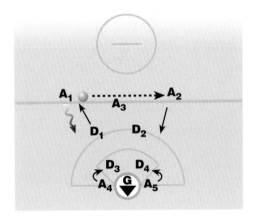

1. Set up three attackers (A1, A2, A3) at the 30-yard line or higher.
2. Two defenders (D1, D2) stand near the 15-yard line.
3. Two attackers (A4, A5) and two defenders (D3, D4) begin at the top of the 12-meter fan.
4. The play starts with one of the attackers at the 30-yard line who is closest to a sideline (A1) bringing the ball down the field.
5. The two lower attackers (A4, A5) must get to the crease while seeing the ball. This brings their defenders (D3, D4) with them and creates space for the ball carrier.
6. The ball carrier (A1) attacks the goal and forces a defender to commit. She then looks to the open player on the back side (A2). The middle attacker (A3) must get below the ball as it is moving down the field and mustn't stay on the same plane as the ball carrier.
7. The ball carrier (A1) can look to pass to the middle attacker (A3) if she gets a step on her defender.
8. The attackers want to maintain their spacing and move the ball to the open players, looking for a shot as quickly as possible.
9. Another option is for the low attacker on the same side as the ball (A4) to pop out and receive a pass. She can dodge or look for cutters from up top. The middle attacker should look to set picks or pop to the ball.
10. Drill continues until each player has had several turns at each position, about 10 to 12 minutes.

The five-on-four also occurs regularly in girls' lacrosse and often presents itself after a foul is called in the offensive half of the field or out of a true fast-break situation in transition play. Again, notice that the low attackers want to get to the goal line extended, by the crease, to give as much space as possible to the ball carrier and make the slide very long for the defenders. The ball carrier should bring the ball down one side of the field to open up the player on the back side as the defense shifts to the ball side. The middle attacker must maintain her spacing (by not getting too deep into the 8-meter arc) and mustn't allow one defender to play two attackers.

Breakout 05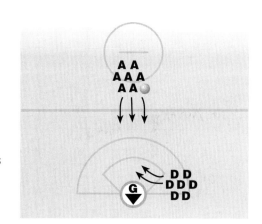

Purpose: To challenge attackers to recognize when they are up or down a player (or two) and react accordingly.	**Number of Players:** 15 (7 attackers, 7 defenders, 1 goalie) **Equipment:** 1 goal, 1 practice jersey per player, 7 balls

1. Group seven attackers near the 30-yard line. They should all be wearing the same color jersey. With seven attackers, there will be seven "sets" to the drill, with one ball per set.
2. Group seven defenders at the 10-yard line, off to one side of the goal. They wear contrasting jerseys to set them apart from the attackers.
3. Each team determines how many players they'll send out for each set. Determine how long the sets will be at the beginning of the drill—perhaps 30 or 45 seconds. Teams can deploy seven players only once, six players only once, five players only once, and so on.
4. For example, on the whistle the attacking team decides that they're sending out three players for the first set (one of whom has the ball).
5. The defensive team decides that they're sending out five players.
6. The first set would be three attackers versus five defenders. (The offense may not send out three again, and the defense may not send out five again.)
7. The offense earns a point if they score within the allotted time (30 or 45 seconds, or whatever time you've selected).
8. The defense earns a point if they get possession of the ball and clear it past the 25-yard line within the allotted amount of time.
9. If time runs out before the attack scores or before the defense clears the ball, no point is awarded.

Breakout is a competitive game that challenges the attackers to recognize whether they are a player up or a player down. In this drill they may find themselves a couple of players up or a couple of players down! No matter what level of players you have (beginner, intermediate, or advanced), this is a fun, competitive game that the girls love to play. Remember to keep track of how many points each team earns to determine the winning team at the end of the drill.

OFFENSIVE DRILLS

World Cup 06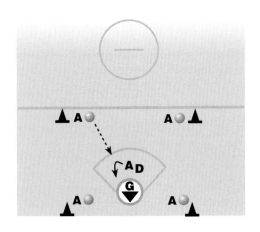

Purpose: To develop the technique of catching and releasing a quick shot under moderate gamelike pressure.	**Number of Players:** 7 (5 attackers, 1 defender, 1 goalie) **Equipment:** 1 goal, 4 cones, 4 balls

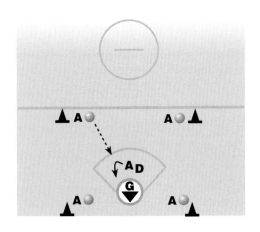

1. Place four cones in a square around the 8-meter arc.
2. One attacker, with a ball, stands at each cone.
3. An attacker and a defender are inside the 8-meter arc.
4. The inside attacker tries to get a feed from each of the outside attackers and get a shot off immediately.
5. The inside attacker should try to take her defender away from where she wants to receive the first feed and then use a quick change of direction to cut diagonally back to the ball and shoot. Diagonal cuts to the ball will allow the attacker inside the 8-meter arc to protect her stick from the defender by shielding it with her body. The attacker doesn't want to have to dodge the defender once she receives the ball; her objective is to catch it on the move and shoot quickly.
6. The inside defender should try to keep the attacker moving in one direction so the goalie knows where the shot will come from, and force an off-angle shot. She should maintain good body position and look to block a shot when possible.
7. The feeders at each cone must be ready to send the ball in to the cutting attacker as soon as her stick is available.
8. Drill continues until each player has had several turns at each position, about 10 to 12 minutes.

Variation: Add another attacker and defender to the inside of the 8-meter arc for two-on-two play. Attackers will try to use picks and take advantage of double-team situations. Defenders will communicate with each other, talk through the picks, and execute effective double teams.

Half-Field Scramble 07

Purpose: To develop transition play (offensive) and to clear the ball under pressure (defensive).

Number of Players: All, in two teams, 1 goalie
Equipment: 1 goal, 1 practice jersey per player, 1 bucket of balls

1. Divide the team in half and have each squad wear jerseys in a different color. You can mix up the players (remember the philosophy of the complete player), or you can put attackers against defenders.
2. Group the attackers at the 50-yard line.
3. Group the defenders on either sideline.
4. The balls are with a coach at the 50-yard line. The coach calls out the number of players to participate in the drill (for example, six-on-six), rolls out a ball, and blows the whistle. The corresponding number of players take the field, going after the ground ball.
5. If the attackers get the ball, they attack the goal cage, pushing a fast break (if available) or falling into settled offensive play.
6. If the defenders get the ball, they must send the ball back to their goalie and then clear it past the restraining line.
7. While the defenders are trying to clear the ball, the attackers are riding them, or pressuring them so they can't clear the ball easily. In the ride, the attackers are trying to cause a turnover and go to the goal.
8. Any number of players can be called out: five-on-five, six-on-six, or seven-on-seven. You can also call out an eight-on-eight or a nine-on-nine, which gives your players practice at communicating and sending only seven attackers across the restraining line.
9. Drill continues for 10 to 12 minutes.

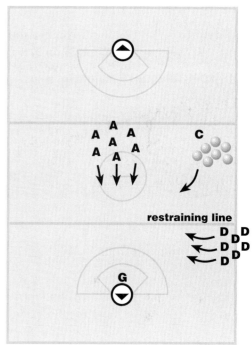

restraining line

Center Draw 08

Purpose: To develop techniques for the center draw and the ability to direct the ball to specific areas at the draw.	**Number of Players:** All, in groups of 3 **Equipment:** Several balls per group

1. Set up the players at a line on the field, making sure sticks are parallel to the ground and the ball is correctly placed in the stick pockets.
2. Once sticks are set, the coach backs away and then blows the whistle to simulate the start of the draw.
3. The players practice getting under the ball by rotating their wrists. They practice timing the sound of the whistle, different stances, and positioning their feet in different ways to enhance their draw techniques. They practice drawing straight up and boxing out to gain possession of the ball.
4. The coach repeatedly sets up the draw, backs away, and blows the whistle so the players can get many chances to "win" the draw.
5. Drill continues for 10 to 12 minutes.

The center draw is a skill that develops with repetition. It's also a skill that unfortunately is rarely incorporated into daily practice plans. Initially have all your players get into groups of three and practice taking the center draw, with one player setting up the draw and the other two executing it. (See pages 29–30 and 65–66 for how to set up a center draw.) Evaluate each of the groups, as you may discover a player you hadn't realized is quite successful at the draw. Once you establish which players you wish to take the center draw in your games, set up this drill a few minutes before, during, or after practice to give your players the repetition they need to develop their own center draw techniques.

Variations: Add pairs of players around the players taking the center draw so they can practice fighting for the ball as it goes up in the air. They should practice boxing out their opponent by stepping diagonally in front of and across their opponent's body and then holding their position to go for the ball.

OFFENSIVE DRILLS

CHAPTER 12

Defensive Drills

This chapter provides drills that break down the components of team defense into small parts and progresses to drills that support the entire team executing successfully on defense.

Breaking down your defensive concepts into smaller components allows your players to understand the basics of team defense and build from there. Always remember to have enough practice jerseys to distinguish the offensive players from the defensive players!

Fast Feet with a Check   D1

Purpose: To increase foot speed, improve the ability to slide, and maintain balance when checking.	**Number of Players:** All **Equipment:** None

1. Spread your team out into three lines facing you. Each player has a stick.
2. Sticks should be held straight up and down with players' arms comfortably away from their body. Players should be in their defensive stance: their weight is on the balls of their feet, with their feet about shoulder-width apart and slightly offset; their knees are bent, as if in a seated position; and they are leaning slightly forward.
3. On the whistle, players move from foot to foot as quickly as possible (as if they were running in place) while keeping their heads up and body weight balanced.
4. Have players execute fast feet for 10 seconds. Then point in a direction for players to slide.

DEFENSIVE DRILLS

5. Slides must be made with short, quick steps, not long, off-balance strides.
6. On your single whistle players are to check and release, snapping the sticks down and back up again quickly in midair, as if they were checking an opponent's stick. Players must keep their head up and their eyes on you to see when you change the direction of the slides.
7. Do this for 30 seconds and then give the players a chance to shake out their legs. Repeat three times.

Players' sticks must remain straight up and down. Players must remain in a seated, balanced position. Checks must be quick and short; there are no big swings.

One-on-One in Grid D2

Purpose: To develop the fundamentals of individual defense.	**Number of Players:** 2 (1 attacker, 1 defender)
	Equipment: 4 cones, 1 ball

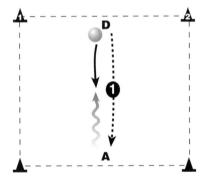

1. Use four cones to create a 15-by-15-yard grid.
2. The defender starts with the ball on one side of the grid and passes to the attacker on the opposite side of the grid.
3. The defender tries to prevent the attacker from dodging or running the ball across the defender's line (the space between cones 1 and 2).
4. Once the attacker catches the ball, it's a one-on-one inside the grid.
5. Play stops when the attacker makes it across the defender's line, or when the defender successfully checks the ball away or forces the attacker outside the grid.
6. Be sure to set up multiple grids so the entire team can participate in this drill at the same time.
7. Drill continues until each player has had several turns at each position, about 10 to 12 minutes.

The defender must approach the ball carrier quickly and at an angle that takes away her strong hand (so as to not let her dodge to either side of the defender). As the defender gets within a stick and arm's length away, she must break down her steps (in her defensive stance) so she doesn't overrun the attacker. The defender is trying to slow down the ball carrier and force her out of the box.

Mark-Up D3

Purpose: To improve defenders' ability to communicate and mark-up on defense.

Number of Players: 15 (7 attackers, 7 defenders, 1 goalie)
Equipment: 1 goal, 1 practice jersey per player, 7 balls

1. Seven defenders stand near the top of the 12-meter fan, all facing each other with their eyes closed (no peeking!).
2. Seven attackers are above the restraining line, in a cluster.
3. On the whistle, the attackers attack the goal with one ball, and the defenders have to communicate which player they have and where the ball is.
4. Play continues until a goal is scored or the defense gains possession of the ball and clears it past the restraining line.

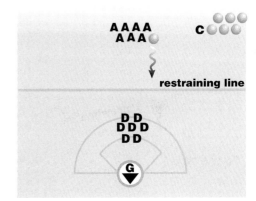

As the ball moves, defenders must be able to adjust their positions on the player they are marking so they can continue to see both the ball and the player. They must learn to back up a step or two to increase their angle in order to see both ball and player and to avoid getting "backdoored," or cut off from behind. The defender on the ball should be yelling, "I've got ball!" continuously so her teammates know where the ball is at all times.

Variation: Have only five or six attackers play against seven defenders so that the defense can work on double-teaming and pressuring the ball.

DEFENSIVE DRILLS

Box Double Team D4

Purpose: To teach effective double-team positioning in a confined area.

Number of Players: 4 (2 attackers, 2 defenders)

Equipment: 4 cones, 1 ball

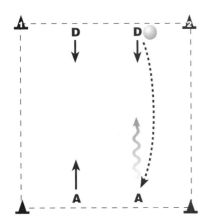

1. Use four cones to create a 15-by-15-yard grid.
2. There are two defenders (one with a ball) on one side of the grid, and two attackers on the other side of the grid, facing each other.
3. Play begins with one of the defenders passing the ball to one of the attackers.
4. Once an attacker catches the ball, the defenders leave their line and work together to prevent the attackers from dodging or passing across the defensive line (between cones 1 and 2).
5. One defender plays the ball, while the other defender tries to play her attacker at an angle to help her fellow defender. The on-ball defender tries to bring her attacker to the off-ball defender for a double team.
6. Play ends when the attackers successfully get the ball across the defensive line, when the defenders force an attacker outside the box, or when the defenders are able to take the ball away from an attacker with an effective double team.

This drill emphasizes the need for defenders to work together to achieve a double team. The on-ball defender is responsible for containing the ball carrier, slowing her down, and directing her toward the second defender. The off-ball defender is responsible for covering the passing lane to the second attacker and for closing the double team when appropriate.

Defending the Three-on-Two D5

Purpose: To develop sliding techniques and communication between defenders when they are down a player.

Number of Players: 6 (3 attackers, 2 defenders, 1 goalie)

Equipment: 1 goal, 1 practice jersey per player, 1 bucket of balls

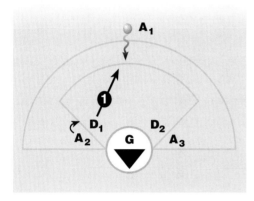
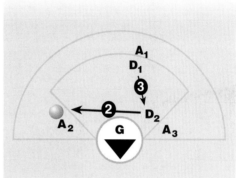

1. In a three-on-two situation, when the ball is near the top of the 12-meter fan, the defender on the ball carrier's strong side (D1) should slide, with her stick in the passing lane of the player she just left, calling "I've got ball!" (left diagram).
2. The opposite defender (D2) must be in position to see the ball and her player and must anticipate the pass to the low player (A2) her teammate just left.
3. As the ball is in the air, the lower defender (D2) steps to the inside of the 8-meter arc and slides across the cage with her stick in the passing lane, taking away the center of the cage (right diagram).
4. The defender who slid initially (D1) must drop-step into the 8-meter arc toward the open attacker (A3), leading with her stick up and in the passing lane, and watches two players until the recovering defender gets into position.
5. Drill continues until each player has had several turns at each position, about 10 to 12 minutes.

When the defense is a player down, their main objective is to slow down the ball enough for their recovering defender to get back into position. The defense wants to force the offense to pass the ball; the more they pass, the more opportunity for error on their part. Timing is important. If the defense slides too early, the offense will have too much space to work with.

Defending the Four-on-Three **D6**

Purpose: To develop the ability of defenders to recognize when they are down a player and to slide correctly to slow down the ball.

Number of Players: 8 (4 attackers, 3 defenders, 1 goalie)

Equipment: 1 goal, 1 practice jersey per player, 1 bucket of balls

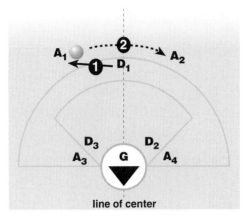

line of center

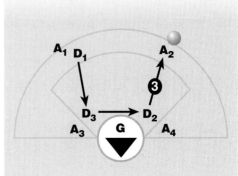

1. When the defense is a player down, it should be as compact as possible. In a four-on-three it should form a triangle. Have one defender (D1) stand at the top of the 12-meter fan and two defenders (D2, D3) in the 8-meter arc, just in front of the goal.
2. Two attackers (A1, A2) stand just outside the 12-meter fan, and two additional attackers (A3, A4) stand along the goal line extended, just outside the 8-meter arc.
3. The defender (D1) at the top of the 12-meter fan must play the ball carrier (A1) between the 8-meter arc and the 12-meter fan. The general rule for positioning is that defenders should slide in the opposite direction of the path of the ball (left diagram).
4. The on-ball defender (D1) must play the ball between the 8-meter arc and the 12-meter fan, forcing the ball carrier (A1) away from the line of center. D1 should not play the ball outside of the 12-meter fan.
5. When the ball is passed to player A2, the defender D1 must turn inside to see the ball and slide down the back side with her stick up and in a passing lane (right diagram).
6. The low player opposite the ball carrier (D2) should anticipate the pass to the open attacker A2 and should slide up, with her stick in a passing lane, while the ball is in the air. She should be aware of shooting space and the 3-second rule.
7. The low player on the same side as the ball (D3) must react to the pass up top. As the pass is made, she must prepare to slide across the crease,

watching shooting space. She must slide to the attacker's stick, *not* her body, as the attacker will most likely curl up to the ball. If the defender slides to the attacker's stick, she will not get beat over the top (toward the middle of the 8-meter arc). If she slides to the attacker's body, she will most likely get beat over the top as the attacker curls up to the ball.

8. The defenders' objective is to slow down the attack so their recovering defender can get in. By making the attackers pass the ball, there is more room for them to make a mistake and create a defensive stop.

9. A3 and A4 maintain the box formation to make it difficult for the defenders to slide.

10. The goalie communicates to the defense throughout the drill, telling them where to slide.

11. Drill continues until each player has had several turns at each position, about 10 to 12 minutes.

Defending the Five-on-Four D7

Purpose: To develop sliding techniques and communication between defenders in a five-on-four situation.	**Number of Players:** 10 (5 attackers, 4 defenders, 1 goalie) **Equipment:** 1 goal, 1 practice jersey per player, 1 bucket of balls

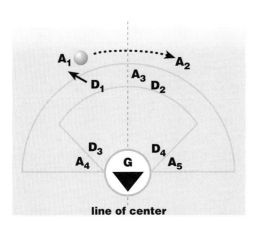

line of center

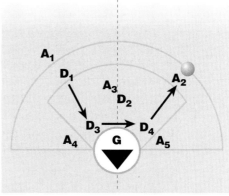

1. When the defense is a player down, it should be as compact as possible. In a five-on-four the defense should form a box. Have two defenders (D1, D2) stand between the 8-meter arc and the 12-meter fan and two defenders (D3, D4) in the 8-meter arc, just in front of the goal.

2. Three attackers (A1, A2, A3) stand just outside the 12-meter fan, and two additional attackers (A4, A5) stand along the goal line extended, just outside the 8-meter arc.

3. The on-ball defender (D1) must play the ball between the 8-meter arc and the 12-meter fan, forcing the ball carrier (A1) away from the line of center. D1 should not play the ball outside of the 12-meter fan because this will make the slides very long and give the attackers more space to work with.

4. The high off-ball defender (D2) must move to the middle if the middle attacker (A3) stays high (left diagram). If the middle attacker (A3) drifts low, D2 must stay on her. As the ball is passed, D4 slides up to A2 with her stick in the passing lane (right diagram).

5. The low back-side defender (D3) should slide in and over to A5. She must be aware of the low back-side attacker, the 3-second rule, and shooting space.

6. The high off-ball defender (D1) must drop-step to the inside of the 8-meter arc (seeing the ball) and slide down to A4. This will leave the attacker farthest from the ball and goal (A1) open.

7. A4 and A5 stay low, waiting to move into open space when their defender slides.

8. The goalie is communicating with her defenders throughout the drill, telling them where to slide.

9. Drill continues for 10 to 12 minutes.

Cross the Line D8

Purpose: To teach how to step up and contain an attack player.	**Number of Players:** All, in pairs
	Equipment: 2 cones, 1 ball per pair

1. One partner in each pair has a ball.
2. Each pair finds a line on the field to work with. If there are no lines on the field, set up two cones, 10 yards apart, for each pair.
3. The player with the ball tries to move across the line. The defender tries to step up and prevent her from doing so.
4. Defenders must stay in their defensive stance, keep their stick up, and take small, quick steps when they slide to prevent the attacker from crossing the line.
5. Players switch roles after 1 minute.
6. Drill continues for 10 to 12 minutes.

Defensive Clearing D9

Purpose: To teach a basic pattern for clearing the ball out of the defensive end.

Number of Players: 8 (4 defenders, 3 midfielders, 1 goalie)

Equipment: 1 goal, 1 bucket of balls

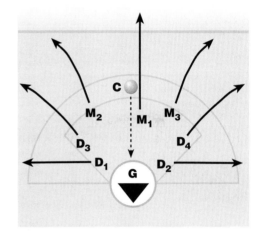

1. Set up four defenders and three midfielders as if in settled defensive play in the 8-meter arc.
2. A coach has a ball at the top of the 8-meter arc and shoots it at the goalie's stick.
3. The goalie saves the shot and calls "Break!" to get the defense breaking into their clearing pattern.
4. Two defenders (D1, D2) break low as quick outlets for the goalie, two defenders (D3, D4) cut up and then curl out toward the sideline (at about the 20-yard line), one midfielder (M1) cuts straight up the field (to open up the center of the field), and the remaining two midfielders (M2, M3) cut up and away toward the sideline at about the 30-yard line.
5. Players must watch the ball and be ready for a pass as they are breaking into their pattern. They must be aware of an offensive player dropping off onto the goalie, which leaves a defensive player open for the clear. Once the initial cuts are made, players must recut on diagonals while maintaining good spacing.
6. Play continues until the defense clears the ball past the 30-yard line or until your whistle.
7. Drill continues for 10 to 12 minutes.

DEFENSIVE DRILLS

Check Me If You Can D10

Purpose: To teach proper checking technique with an emphasis on "check and release."	**Number of Players:** All, in pairs
	Equipment: 1 ball per pair

1. Partners face each other. One player in each pair has a ball.
2. The player with the ball holds her stick out in front (with her top hand placed about halfway down the stick) and parallel to the ground and cradles from side to side, trying to avoid the defender's check. She wants to bait the defender into checking and then move her stick quickly out of the way.
3. The defender times the ball carrier's cradle and patiently waits to check. Her top hand is placed one-third of the way down the stick, and her feet are offset for balance. The player checks her partner by snapping her stick down, aiming for the corner of the ball carrier's stick to dislodge the ball.
4. After 5 minutes, have players switch positions. Drill continues for another 5 minutes.

This drill emphasizes staying balanced when checking and the importance of a quick check and release with no backswing. Players are encouraged to be patient and wait for the right opportunity to check, which develops control and good decision making.

CHAPTER 13

Goalkeeping Concepts and Drills

Our guest contributor for this chapter is Trish Dabrowski, NCAA Division I Goalkeeper of the Year in 2002. A graduate of Loyola College in Maryland, Trish is a three-time All-American. She was Colonial Athletic Association conference MVP in 1999 and was conference defensive player of the year and Loyola College women's lacrosse MVP in 2002. She is now an assistant women's lacrosse coach at Johns Hopkins University.

"With the lessons I've learned over the past years and the passion I have for the sport of lacrosse, it's time to give back what has been given to me," Trish says. "So, let's talk goalkeeping!"

Who's Right for the Job?

For Trish, goalkeeping was 90 percent mental and 10 percent physical. So it stands to reason that a successful goalkeeper needs a mental toughness that borders on arrogance when she puts on the pads and steps onto the field.

It's the mental game that takes the most time to develop: not being afraid of the ball, keeping your head up, and not getting down on yourself when balls go in the goal. Like it or not, goalkeepers get scored on. It's important to remind your young players of this simple fact of goalie life.

Important physical traits include quick hands and feet in order to save the ball and recover for second or third shots, hand-eye coordination to react successfully to oncoming shots, and an all-over agility to allow a goalkeeper to be mobile outside the crease, whether it's running down ground balls or making interceptions. Finally, a goalkeeper must be able to communicate, loudly verbalizing the position of the ball to help the defensive unit work as one.

Equipment

Make sure that the equipment neither weighs down the athlete nor inhibits mobility. Properly fitting equipment won't impede a goalie's athleticism—although even the best goalie equipment will tend to envelop and overpower most players under 12 and turn them into Michelin Man look-alikes. Here's a hint: during practice a goalkeeper should wear more protection than is necessary; during games she should shed anything that's not absolutely required. The rationale: she'll feel freer, but still be safe. A goalkeeper is bound to get hit more in practice because she'll see many more shots than in a game.

The goalie stance.

All goalkeepers must wear an NCAA-approved helmet, mouth guard, separate throat guard, chest protector, and gloves. Thigh and shin pads are mandatory at the youth level. All of this equipment can be purchased at any lacrosse specialty store (see the resources section for suggestions).

Helmet. The helmet should fit comfortably and not be too tight when the chinstrap is connected. The goalkeeper should be looking through the top bar of the helmet. If she's looking anywhere else, she may need another size. Lacrosse manufacturers today make lightweight helmets that are more comfortable to wear. Helmets also come in a variety of fun colors.

Throat guard. Buy only throat protectors specifically made for lacrosse players; stay away from field hockey or ice hockey throat protectors since they are not approved for lacrosse. Throat guards are made of either foam or plastic and should attach easily to the bottom of the helmet by ties or snaps. The foam pad stretches the length of the helmet and covers the entire throat area. The plastic protector hangs from string and is not as wide as the foam guard. Plastic ones tend to move around more and don't cover all of the throat area.

Chest protector. There are dozens of chest protector styles for goalies. Beginning players should consider purchasing the chest protector that includes side or rib protection. The chest protector should start at the neck and cover that area where the neck and collarbone begin, including the entire chest and stomach areas. Make sure it's not too big, too loose, or too tight, and that it allows mobility.

Gloves. There are gloves made specifically for goalkeepers with metal bits in the fingers and thumb area. The gloves should be padded, but not be too big. The goalkeeper needs a full range of motion of her hands and wrists. No women's lacrosse goalie should be wearing field player gloves.

Thigh pads. Thigh pads have been designed specifically for women's lacrosse goalkeepers. Most are made with spandex and have pads inserted in the proper areas. They should also include a pelvic protector. If one is not provided in the pads, purchase one separately. No goalkeeper should be wearing ice hockey pads; they are too thick and limit mobility.

Shin pads. Lacrosse manufacturers make custom-molded shin guards, often used for field hockey, that protect the entire shin. Shin guards used by baseball catchers are too big and can limit mobility. Soccer shin guards are adequate, but most do not protect the entire shin area.

Stick. There are a variety of goalie sticks, mesh, and shafts. It's a matter of personal preference which stick a goalie chooses. A hard-mesh pocket takes a lot of time to break in, but most goalkeepers today prefer the hard mesh because it allows them to create pockets they feel comfortable with when playing. The ball also sticks better to the hard mesh, which can result in better possession in the pocket. However, hard mesh tends to expand when it gets wet and the pocket can get bigger. When it dries, it shrinks and gets smaller, which can adversely affect a goalie's ability to clear.

A soft mesh pocket tends to create a very low pocket close to the ball stopper. When this happens the ball can get stuck, making it more difficult to clear the ball.

Stick shafts are usually made of titanium, aluminum, or alloy. They vary in style, width, and feel and range in price, weight, and color.

A side view of the proper goalie stance. Notice her positioning slightly in front of the goal line with her arms comfortably away from her body.

Fundamentals
Stance and Hand Positioning

A goalkeeper's stance and hand positioning are as important as a tennis player's volley and serve. She should work on these skills from the outset.

In the stance, the goalkeeper needs to be on the balls of her feet (not on the toes) with her knees slightly bent. Her feet should be shoulder-width apart, and her weight should be balanced on the balls of her feet. Her back should be upright, and both arms should be away from the body, yet inside the goalkeeper's body frame, which means that the stick, elbows, arms, and feet should stay within the width of her shoulders for every shot. On some occasions, a goalkeeper may have to reach outside her frame for a wide or high shot.

The arms should not be fully extended but bent enough so there is significant space between

the body and the stick. The goalkeeper's top hand should be at the top of the stick, and the thumb should be lined up with the dominant-side eye. Her bottom hand should be in the middle of the shaft, aligned with the hip. The goalkeeper's stance and hand positioning should feel comfortable, relaxed, and balanced.

Movement in the Crease and Developing Angles

Among the most challenging aspects of goalkeeping to teach are moving in the crease and developing angles. Both take time and repetition to master. Until recently, goalkeepers were supposed to play either a *house* or a *semicircle* style of positioning, which brought the goalkeeper higher in the goal, or farther away from the goal line.

But changes in stick technology have affected the throwing speed of sticks and increased shot placement and accuracy. This has caused goalkeepers to change their style of play to a *semiflat* style, which can be described as a step back toward the goal line, which gives the goalie more time to react to the ball. The initial step coming off the pipe from the goal line extended is a flat, square step about a foot above the goal line. The first step, from the pipe, should not be out and up, which moves the goalie too high in the goal. This is the old style of play and does not allow as much reaction time as the new method.

The objective of both older-style positions was to take away the angle of the shooter. But with field players becoming smarter and shots coming harder and faster, this high positioning allows for less reaction time. Also, sticks now are made so that shooters can extend out farther to release shots. If the goalkeeper is in a house position, these shots could go right around the goalkeeper. The semiflat style allows goalies to play deeper in the goal, providing more time to see and react to the ball.

Have the goalkeeper practice moving from pipe to pipe—from one side of the goal to the other—with her eyes closed while you instruct her to stay back and flat.

It's vital for the goalkeeper to stay square to the ball, meaning she should keep her hips, shoulders, and feet balanced and lined up directly with the ball. A goalie's hips should be balanced and even with the shooter. She should never open her hips; this exposes more surface area of the goal. With open hips, the initial step is back instead of up and out to the ball. Staying square to the ball and shooter

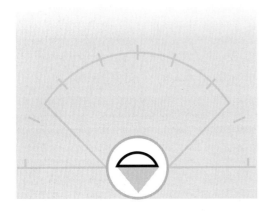

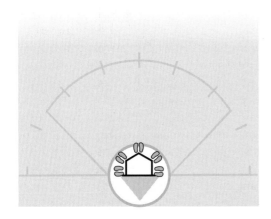

The semicircle (top) and house (bottom) methods limit the goalkeeper's time to react to the shot because of high positioning in the goal.

allows a goalkeeper to make saves with her body even if her stick happens to miss.

Another key to keeping the correct angle in the goal is to stay patient and stay back on the semiflat position until the shot is released. When a goalkeeper starts to creep out or get "happy feet," it becomes easier for a good field player to fake and shoot right around her. The easiest and most effective way to stay back and patient is for the goalkeeper to tell herself to hold until she sees the release of the ball from the stick.

Making the Save

Take the time to teach this portion of goalkeeping correctly and make sure it's practiced regularly until the goalkeeper understands the skill and technique.

On many occasions, goalkeepers tend to drop their upper body and bend forward at the waist, making them smaller in the goal. Tell your goalkeeper to "stay big" to help her stay in a good vertical position and use whatever height she has to her advantage. Goalkeepers need to look as big as possible while standing in an athletic position.

Make sure that the goalkeeper's stick, arms, elbows, and feet are within her body frame and that she's stepping square to the ball. Her initial step should be up and out to the ball and not back, where she'll tend to open her hips. On the save, tell the goalkeeper to think about the ball splitting her body in half. This technique will help her stay square to the ball on the save.

The term *nose to ball* often is used when watching a ball into the stick. When the goalkeeper's nose follows the ball, her eyes have no choice but to watch the ball as well. This helps the goalkeeper stay focused until the ball is controlled in her stick. The drills section at the end of this chapter has tips for working on this technique. **G6** **G7**

One of the most important things to teach goalies is to *take their hands to the ball*, meaning they should reach or lean for the ball first with their hands, and not lead with their feet. Have goalkeepers overexaggerate taking their hands to the ball until their feet have to catch them before they fall over. Often goalkeepers step with their feet first, which leaves their hands too close to the body, making it difficult to save and control the ball. Goalkeepers should explode and power to the ball with their hands first and with their feet second.

Goalies should step to make a save on a 45-degree angle to cut off the angle of the shot. This step is not a lunge or a hop but a quick two steps. The

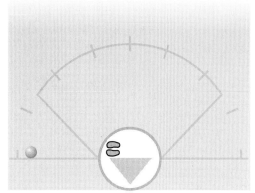

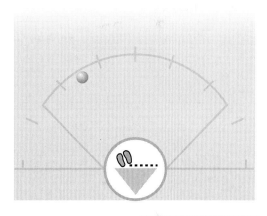

The semiflat style. In the top diagram, the ball is on the goal line extended. The foot closest to the pole should be on the pipe. The other foot should be shoulder-width away. The goalie's stick and hands should be out and away from her body. In the bottom diagram, the ball is between the second and third hash mark. The goalkeeper has moved in a "semiflat" manner, staying square to the ball. The goalkeeper's movement should be along the dashed line as the ball travels across the 8-meter arc.

A goalie holds the pole— stands tight against it—as she anticipates a shot.

trailing foot must come up for balance and helps control the ball on the save. Some goalkeepers may power or explode to the ball so strongly that their momentum may carry them to a hop step. There is nothing wrong with this, but they shouldn't bring their feet together at the end. To make sure they step on a 45-degree angle, they should be able to walk in a straight line backward and touch their butt to the pipe.

Whatever side the ball is shot on, the goalkeeper's first step is with the foot on that side. Thus, if the ball is shot anywhere on the right side, the goalkeeper needs to step with her right foot first. If the ball is shot anywhere on the left side of the body, the goalkeeper needs to step with her left foot first. The goalie should remember to take her hands to the ball first and then let her body follow. She should watch the ball all the way into the stick, give with the ball, and keep the body square and behind the ball.

A good check for correct positioning is to have the goalkeeper line up her belly button with the ball. This applies to all shots. She should always line up with the ball, rather than with the player who is shooting.

The goalkeeper should never take her eyes off the ball. She must watch it all the way into her stick. Goalkeepers should not punch at the ball or catch and cradle the ball. The goalkeeper's job is to save it. This requires soft hands. As the goalkeeper reaches out to save the ball, she should pretend that the ball is an egg. As she watches the ball into her stick, she should give with it in front of her body, keeping her eye on the ball the entire time.

Breaking Down Some Different Shots

What follows is a breakdown of various shots and the proper methods by which to save them.

Shots from goalkeeper's right side, high. From the stance position, the goalkeeper's top hand needs to go out to the ball while she steps with the right foot and follows with the left foot. Feet are shoulder-width apart. The goalkeeper goes after the ball with her hands, while keeping her stick directly in front of her body. She shouldn't save the ball on the side or at the shoulder but directly in front of her face. She should punch out the bottom hand and point the bottom of the shaft upfield. The bottom arm should be fully extended to help the goalkeeper give with the ball and allow the ball to sit nicely in the pocket. If the goalkeeper goes after the ball and her stick is vertical, the ball will hit the pocket and fall out.

Shots from goalkeeper's left side, high. From the stance position, the goalkeeper needs to bring her stick out and over to the opposite side of her body.

The incorrect way is what we call a windshield wiper motion, where the arms cross and form an X. This means the goalkeeper didn't take her hands out to the ball. She should explode to the ball with her hands first, and this time the left foot steps to the ball with the right foot trailing. The same give-and-step motion applies.

Shots from goalkeeper's right side, middle. From the stance position, the goalkeeper should bend her knees and save the ball around the hip area. It's important here to get the body behind the ball. When making this save, goalkeepers usually do a good job of taking their hands to the ball but often forget to move their body. They should make sure the ball is still splitting their body in half and that their stick is not outside their body frame on the save. They need to step with their right foot first and follow with their left foot trailing.

Shots from goalkeeper's left side, middle. The dip save and the flip save are two of the most difficult saves to make because sometimes goalkeepers react high and sometimes they flip the stick underneath. There's an easy-to-recite rhyme that helps goalkeepers to react to the ball in the correct way: "From your shoulder to your hip, you *dip* to the ball, and from your hip to your knee, you *flip* to the ball."

The *dip save* is used when the ball is shot between the goalkeeper's shoulder and hip. From the stance position, the goalkeeper should save this ball just like the left-side, high shot. The goalkeeper may have to get a little lower and farther under the ball. All goalies are different, and some can get low enough to save this shot at their knees. If that's the case, there's no choice but to bend at the knees, because there's no way the goalkeeper can get under the ball and make this save by bending at the waist. Getting under the ball means that at the end of the save, the stick should be out in front of the body, and the goalkeeper's body should be underneath and behind the ball.

The *flip save* is used when the ball is shot between the goalkeeper's hip and knees. Remember, all goalies are different. Those who are less flexible may need to make this save when the ball is shot at knee height.

From the stance position, the goalkeeper needs to drop her stick vertically to the ground, making sure it stays within her body frame. Around the knee area, the goalkeeper needs to bring her top hand around so that it ends up as the bottom hand. While dropping the stick vertically, the goalkeeper should be stepping to the ball with her left foot. As she flips the stick around, the trailing foot should be following. Similar to the goalkeeper's right-side, middle save, the ball splits the body in half, and the body should be behind her stick. This is when goalkeepers tend to turn their hips and open up their bodies.

The incorrect way to make this save is to use a windmill motion, or when a goalie starts to bring the stick head around to her knees and ends up bringing the head of her stick outside her body frame. This is the old way to make the save.

Shots from goalkeeper's right side, low. For this save, the goalkeeper uses the flip technique discussed above. Dropping the stick vertically, the goalkeeper flips the stick (when it's at about her shin area), ending with the stick head touching the ground and staying inside the body frame. While dropping the stick, the goalkeeper takes the hands to the ball and steps to the ball with the right foot and the left foot trailing. She should watch the ball all the way into the stick and make sure the stick head does not drop.

After the save, the goalkeeper should look as though she is sitting low in an invisible chair. The body is behind and over the ball, and the "bottom" stick hand is now on top. The goalkeeper points the bottom of her shaft at a 45-degree angle in order to keep the ball in front. As with every save, the ball should split the goalkeeper's body in half. Her feet should end up shoulder-width apart, just wide enough so her legs could make a save if the stick misses.

If a goalkeeper is stepping on her stick, her hands are not far enough away from her body. She shouldn't bend at the waist since that strains the back and slows down reaction time.

Shots from goalkeeper's left side, low. Goalkeepers use the same technique here as for shots from the right side, low. However, when the goalkeeper drops her stick vertically, she needs to step first with her left foot and her right foot trails.

Bounce shots. The goalkeeper should try to save the ball before it bounces. She needs to get her hands out front and to explode to the ball.

Low bounce shots, which are shot closer to the goalie's feet, can be played just like low shots. The goalkeeper should get her hands out front and keep her body low, which means bending the knees, getting over the top of the ball, and watching the ball all the way into the stick.

A goalie defends against a low shot.

With high bounce shots, which are shot just inside the top of the crease, goalies have to watch and track the ball carefully. Quick hand-eye coordination comes in handy here. Most youth goalkeepers play on grass, which makes true bounce shots unlikely. On a turf field, high bounce shots can be truer and a little easier to save. *True* means that on turf, the ball won't take a bad bounce and won't get misdirected. On a grass field, the easiest way to test the grass and the divots in the crease is for the players to take a lot of high bounce shots during the warm-up.

The goalkeeper should make sure her hands are way out in front so that they're almost pulling the body behind the stick. This allows the goalkeeper to make this save with her body if she doesn't get it with her stick.

Keeping her arms in front will help the goalkeeper save the ball at a decent height and before the ball comes up into her.

Shots from in close. In women's lacrosse, goalies need to be prepared for lots of shots in close to the crease. The key to saving these shots is for the goalkeeper to match her stick to the shooter's stick. The goalkeeper should take a small step out to the shooter to cut off the angle of the shot. She shouldn't come rushing out to the shooter because a good shooter would see her coming, throw a fake, and put the ball right around her into the goal. Instead, tell your goalkeeper to be patient and to avoid "happy feet"—moving out to the shooter too early. Goalkeepers need to hold until they see the shooter break her cradle and notice the ball rolling up from the pocket. This is when the goalkeeper takes her step out and matches her stick with the attacker's stick.

8-meter shots. No matter which hash mark the attacker ends up on, the goalkeeper should make sure she has lined up her belly button to the ball. This will keep her aligned and on the correct angle. She should stay patient until the shot is released and then attack it. A more advanced goalkeeper may try to cheat a little to the off-ball side, so as the attacker lines up, she sees a lot of space and net on the goalkeeper's strong stick side. The goalkeeper knows that this is where she wants the player to shoot, and more than likely when the attacker sees all that space, she will shoot there. Since this is the goalkeeper's strong side, it should be a high-percentage save.

Crease rolls. On a crease roll, the ball starts from X (point behind). As the attacker starts to roll and works her way to the center of the goal, it's very important for the goalkeeper to follow the ball, not the player. As soon as the attacker reaches the goal line extended, the goalkeeper should be on her pipe (positioned at the corner of the goal cage). As the attacker starts making her way to the center of the cage, the goalkeeper shouldn't get antsy and move ahead of the attacker. She must stay square to the ball. Her belly button must be lined up to the ball, and she needs to be on the balls of her feet. She keeps her hands out in front and attacks the ball when the attacker releases it.

The worst thing a goalkeeper can do is take herself out of position by creeping out too high. The keys to preventing a goal are staying patient and watching the ball.

Practicing saves is a good way for goalkeepers to warm up. The coach should stand just inside the 8-meter arc and shoot on goal using a variety of shots, from either the center of the arc or moving around inside the arc. Allow the goalkeeper to practice each type of save about 10 times. If the coach or the goalie feels she needs more practice with a particular save, keep sending those until she's comfortable.

The warm-up shouldn't be confused with shooting practice, so refrain from pelting the goalie with hard, fast shots. Do what it takes to build her confidence. End the warm-up on a saved shot—never on one that goes into the goal—and assure the goalie she performed well.

Playing the Ball Behind

Foot positioning is most important when playing the ball behind (when the opposing team has the ball at X). A goalkeeper should never be standing on the goal line or out at the top of the crease. She should be comfortably in the middle of the goal, because if she misses the interception she must turn and be in the correct position to make the save. If the ball is behind low right (see Communication later in this chapter), the goalkeeper should place her right foot a little closer to the goal line while keeping her feet shoulder-width apart and still positioned in the middle of the crease. Ditto for when the ball is behind low left. This time, however, her left foot is slightly higher. The foot closer to the goal line is the foot she will push off when she turns. The goalkeeper should be on the balls of her feet, with her knees slightly bent and her feet shoulder-width apart.

Her bottom hand should be all the way at the bottom of the shaft of her stick. Her pinkie should hang off the bottom of the shaft and wrap underneath the stopper. The top hand should slide to the middle of the shaft. The goalkeeper should never wave the stick above or along the top pipe. This lets the attacker know the goalkeeper is looking to intercept the ball. Nor should her stick be on the ground or out of position to make a save. The stick head should be around her shoulder area. The goalkeeper wants to trick the attacker into thinking she is not looking for an interception.

When intercepting the ball, the goalkeeper uses her bottom hand to power up and reach for the ball. She may be able to intercept anything that goes anywhere over the top pipe and even anything that is close to the side pipes. She shouldn't jump or hop to get the ball. On the reach, her stick should be tilted back a little so the ball will sit nicely in her pocket. She shouldn't try to cradle the ball into the stick; rather, she should let the ball fall in with the give motion.

If the goalkeeper misses the interception, which often happens, she should watch the ball and follow the feed, first with her head and then with her body. A goalkeeper should never turn her back to the ball. When she drops her stick into her normal stance positioning, it shouldn't be so low that she has to bring it back up again. Practice this slowly, but know that in games this turn is quick.

Clearing and Throwing

Clearing the ball is one of the most overlooked skills in a goalkeeper's game. Many times a goalkeeper makes a great save, only to throw away the ball because she couldn't clear it. This is one of the easiest skills to practice; all that is needed is a stick, a ball, and a wall. **G9**

The technique of clearing is similar to a baseball pitch. The pitcher

Left: A goalie reaches back before clearing the ball.

Right: A goalie follows through while clearing the ball.

steps with her opposite foot, points the foot to her intended target, turns her hips, releases the ball, and follows through to her catcher. The same steps should be followed when throwing a lacrosse ball, with a few added elements.

When clearing, the hand positioning on the shaft of the stick is different from that in the standard stance. The top hand must slide down to the middle of the shaft and the bottom hand should be completely at the bottom. This allows the goalkeeper to throw the ball more accurately and maximize distance.

The body acts as if it is pitching a baseball. The goalkeeper should step with the opposite foot and point her toes in the direction in which she wants the ball to go. It's important to keep the arms out and away from the body. When the arms are close to the body, most goalies tend to throw the ball off their shoulder, which does not allow them to throw it very far. On the release, the goalkeeper's arms should be up and away from her body, and the stick should be behind her head. She steps with the opposite foot, turns her hips square, and follows through to the intended target. The follow-through should be across the body—not under the armpit.

Throwing a lacrosse ball requires a push-pull motion. This applies to goalies and field players. All players should make sure they are pushing with their top hand and pulling the shaft with their bottom hand for power and distance. If the ball goes directly to the ground, a player is either pulling the ball too much or her follow-through is toward the ground. If the ball sails over the head of the intended target, she is pushing too much with her top hand. Nice crisp passes require a happy medium of the push and the pull motion.

To become a complete goalkeeper, it's imperative that youth players use both their dominant and nondominant hand. In practice, instruct the goalkeeper to clear the ball with her nondominant hand so that in games she'll feel comfortable switching without thinking twice.

Remember that a goalkeeper has 10 seconds in the crease with the ball before she needs to clear it. This is a lot more time than most goalkeepers think. They should relax and be confident with the ball. Possession, control, and good decision making are crucial to the game. An umpire should be counting out loud how much time a goalkeeper has left in the crease. When the count reaches about eight, the goalkeeper should step outside the crease and look for an open teammate. If an opposing attacker is pressuring her, she should stay inside the crease and walk to the back of the goal cage for a clear.

Goalkeepers have an unlimited amount of time outside of the crease to clear. A new rule allows a goalkeeper to reenter the crease with the ball just one time during a possession. This means that if the goalkeeper saves the ball in the crease and walks out of the crease with the ball, she can't roll the ball back in the crease again.

After the ball is cleared, goalkeepers should be prepared to be a *trail*, or a help option to her teammate with the ball. If the teammate who recovered the clear gets pressured or needs help, she can throw the ball back to the goalkeeper, who can then either look to switch fields or hold onto the ball until another teammate gets open.

Most young goalkeepers are told not to clear in the middle of the field. This is because if there's a turnover, the opposing team is in perfect position to score. If there is an open teammate in the middle of the field, the goalkeeper should clear to her, making sure it's a crisp, clean pass that can easily be handled. But for the most part, the sides are the safest areas for clears.

Goalkeepers should never force the pass and must be confident when clearing the ball. Some goalkeepers tend to tense up, which causes them to throw bad passes. When a goalkeeper has the ball, her team has possession and the opposing team can't score. Make sure the goalkeeper practices changing the level of her stick. It's necessary to practice overarm, sidearm, and underarm passes. This will help the goalkeeper develop as an athletic and versatile player.

Communication

Communication is a must for a goalkeeper. It's important for a goalkeeper to talk to her defense on the field. A lacrosse goalkeeper is the "quarterback" and eyes of the field since she can see the entire field. The team relies on the direction and leadership of the goalkeeper. Not only does this allow the goalkeeper to get comfortable with her defensive unit and team, but it also allows the team to feel comfortable with the goalkeeper.

In youth lacrosse, remember that the goalkeeper's focus and concentration on the ball is her number-one priority. Talking can increase after she achieves a comfort level performing her main job.

A goalkeeper should do most of her talking when the opposing goalkeeper or team has the ball. "Goalie ball!" is usually called to let the team and defense know that the opposing team is preparing to clear the ball. When the opposing goalie releases the ball, "Ball out!" is usually called. Most talking is done in the defensive 30—from the restraining line to the goal.

When the ball is in your team's defensive area, ball positions are recognized. Communicating about the position of the ball not only helps the defense, but also allows the goalkeeper to stay focused on the ball. See the sidebar for a list of goalie terms.

Goalie Terms

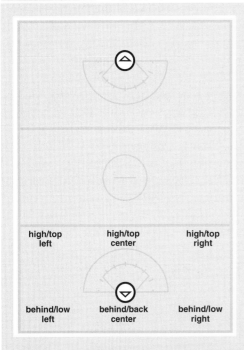

high/top left · high/top center · high/top right

behind/low left · behind/back center · behind/low right

Ball's high/top left
Ball's high/top center
Ball's high/top right
Ball's behind/low left
Ball's behind/back center
Ball's behind/low right

When these terms are called out by the goalie, they help the defense know where the ball is on the field and what direction it is coming from. Here are some other terms.

Check: When the ball is fed anywhere into the 8-meter arc, this term alerts the defense to close the defensive space on the player with the ball so she doesn't get a good shot.

Ball down: When the ball is anywhere on the ground.

Break or clear: Either term lets the defense know the goalkeeper has the ball and is looking to move it up the field.

Ball positions in goalkeeper's defensive 30, the 30 yards from the restraining line to the goal. Low left and low right are a goalkeeper's preference and can be reversed. To make it easier for younger players, call the ball positions this way. Defensive players also should understand this terminology.

Play outside the Crease

A favorite pastime of world-class goalkeepers (like Trish!) is to intercept lazy passes from the attackers around the crease, intercept feeds in the middle, or come up with possession for their team by running down ground balls or missed shots behind the cage. Big plays like these can easily change the momentum of the game in favor of your team.

When playing outside the crease, a goalkeeper should be aggressive and not worry about making a mistake. Once she makes a decision to go, she should *go*, with no hesitation. A goalkeeper needs to know the right time to go and know her distances and speed. Goalkeepers should be encouraged to take risks during practices so they can learn to determine the right times to go and where they feel the most comfortable outside the crease.

Practice and repetition are the keys to goalkeeping. The more shots a goalkeeper can see on a regular basis, inside and outside practice, the better she'll become at goalkeeping. Whatever time and energy a player puts into goalkeeping is what she'll get out of it.

With some conscientious coaching, a goalkeeper will desire to be in the goal and will love and welcome the challenge it offers. She'll be able to show emotion when a big save or a big play is made. She'll learn to enjoy the sound of the ball hitting the mesh as she saves a shot and wins the game.

Coach your young goalkeepers not to worry about the last goal scored. They shouldn't hang their heads, or blame or yell at their teammates. Help them recognize the mistakes and the shots that should have been saved and separate them from the mistakes made by the defense.

Encourage a goalkeeper to prepare for the next shot by telling herself, "I've got the next one!"

Note: You can modify any of the drills that use sticks by having the goalkeeper use a field player stick, which helps the goalkeeper move more quickly to the ball. The smaller field player stick also forces the goalkeeper to watch the ball all the way into the stick and to get her body behind the ball. Remember that in order for the ball to stay in the stick, the goalie must give with it. She should give in front of her body and not to the side.

Drills

Jump Rope G1

Purpose: To develop quick feet and have a good warm-up before getting into the goal.	**Number of Players:** 1 goalie **Equipment:** 1 jump rope

1. Have the goalkeeper arrive at practice at least 10 minutes before the regular starting time.
2. She warms up by jumping rope for 10 minutes.

Quick Feet G2

Purpose: To develop balance and a quick, explosive step.	**Number of Players:** 1 goalie **Equipment:** 1 goalie stick

1. The goalkeeper lays her stick on the ground in front of her with the shaft running left to right.
2. She stands behind the stick in a good stance, with her feet shoulder-width apart and her weight on the balls of her feet. She keeps her hands up and away from her body as if in her ready stance, and keeps her head up.
3. She jumps over the shaft of the stick and lands on both feet together. The movement should be quick and explosive. As soon as she lands on the other side, she jumps back with both feet. She repeats this action for 30 seconds.
4. Next, the goalkeeper again lines up behind the shaft as in step 2.
5. She jumps over the shaft, landing first with her right foot and then with her left. Both feet should now be over the shaft of the stick, and the stick should be behind her.
6. She jumps back to the starting position, landing first with her right foot and then with her left. She repeats this action for 30 seconds and then repeats the entire sequence one more time.

Juggling G3

Purpose: To develop hand-eye coordination.	**Number of Players:** 1 goalie
	Equipment: 3 tennis or lacrosse balls

1. The goalkeeper starts off with two balls, juggling them in one hand.
2. She holds the two balls in her dominant hand. She tosses one ball up in the air, not too high, and when that ball is on its way down, she tosses the other ball up in the air. She repeats this same process for 1 to 2 minutes.
3. When she is comfortable juggling two balls, have her add the third ball and use two hands.

Hand-Slap Game G4

Purpose: To develop hand-eye coordination, peripheral vision, and quick reaction time.	**Number of Players:** 2 goalies
	Equipment: None

1. Goalkeeper 1 extends her hands in front of her with both palms touching.
2. Goalkeeper 2 stands in front of goalkeeper 1 and places her hands on top of the hands of goalkeeper 1.
3. Goalkeeper 1 pulls her hands out and tries to slap the top of goalkeeper 2's hands before goalkeeper 2 pulls her hands away. If she is successful, she keeps going. Once goalkeeper 1 misses, her hands go on the bottom, and goalkeeper 2 attempts to slap goalkeeper 2's hands.
4. Drill continues for 3 to 4 minutes.

   Variation: Both goalkeepers try to slap each other's knees while trying to protect their own. Players should stay low and on the balls of their feet with quick movement.

Added Pressure G5

Purpose: To develop a level of comfort when outside the crease and under pressure.

Number of Players: 2 goalies, 1 coach
Equipment: Full goalie equipment, 1 stick, 1 ball

1. The coach stands in the middle of the 8-meter arc with a stick and a ball.
2. One goalkeeper (G1) positions herself at the top of the crease, looking at the goalkeeper in the goal (G2), who is in her ready stance, preparing to save a shot.
3. The coach rolls the ball behind the crease to either side. G2 chases the ball behind the goal cage and clears it to the coach. Once G2 has the ball, she needs to relax, stay composed, and make a good clear to the coach.
4. G1 adds pressure by trying to prevent G2 from recovering the ground ball.
5. The coach randomly varies throwing to the right and the left so that G2 gets practice using both the right and left hand to clear the ball.
6. After 5 or 6 minutes, have the goalkeepers switch positions, and repeat.

Tennis or Lacrosse Ball Toss G6

Purpose: To develop the 45-degree angle step while focusing on exploding to the ball.

Number of Players: 2 goalies
Equipment: 2 pairs of goalie gloves, 10 tennis or lacrosse balls

1. Goalkeepers face one another about 6 yards apart. G1 starts with the ball; G2 is in a good stance position with her hands away from her body.
2. G1 tosses the ball in the air with her hands to the high side of the dominant hand of G2, who tries to take both hands to the ball and step up and out on a 45-degree angle.
3. G2 now tosses the ball to G1. Each player should make 7 to 10 saves.

   This drill is a good one for beginners, but it's also useful for more advanced goalies as a warm-up. Make sure players toss the ball underhand and don't throw overhand. Players should do this drill without a stick, using only their hands.

GOALKEEPING DRILLS

Rapid-Fire with Tennis Balls G7

Purpose: To develop hand-eye coordination and quick reaction time.	**Number of Players:** 1 goalie, 1 coach **Equipment:** 1 tennis racket, 1 bucket of tennis balls

1. The goalkeeper stands in the goal in her ready stance, preparing to save a shot.
2. The coach kneels 3 or 4 yards in front of the goalkeeper with the bucket of tennis balls and the tennis racket.
3. The coach begins hitting the tennis balls at the goal, one after another.
4. The goalkeeper uses her hands to save as many balls as she can.
5. Drill continues for 5 to 6 minutes.

The goalkeeper should save each shot and quickly get set for the next shot. For a beginning goalkeeper, start slowly and progress to hitting the balls more quickly. Make sure the goalkeeper is taking both hands to the ball and getting her body behind it.

Variation: As the goalkeeper becomes more comfortable saving the balls, have her use a field player's stick and then a goalie stick.

Turning to Find the Shot G8

Purpose: To develop the ability to quickly find the ball in preparation for the shot.	**Number of Players:** 1 goalie, 1 coach **Equipment:** Full goalie equipment, 1 stick, 1 bucket of balls

1. The coach stands with a field player stick anywhere around the perimeter of the 8-meter arc.
2. The goalkeeper stands looking at the goal with her back to the coach (the shooter).
3. The coach can move anywhere around the 8-meter arc. When ready to shoot she yells "Shot!" and shoots the ball at the goal.
4. When the goalkeeper hears the coach's signal, she turns herself around and tries to make the save. It doesn't matter which way the goalkeeper turns as long as she gets herself set and in a good position to make the save.
5. The coach should not shoot the ball until the goalkeeper looks set. The coach continues shooting until all the balls in the bucket are gone.

Clearing and Throwing G9

Purpose: To develop accuracy with long passes with the right and left hand.

Number of Players: 1 goalie
Equipment: 1 goalie stick, 1 pair of goalie gloves, 1 bucket of balls

1. The goalkeeper takes a bucket of lacrosse balls out to a goal cage.
2. She moves around the field from the 50-yard line (half field) and below, trying to clear the ball and throw it into the goal cage. The goalkeeper should concentrate on the distance and accuracy of each throw. Have her do this drill on the run.
3. Drill continues for 10 minutes.

Variation: This drill can also be done against a wall. Make a few boxes of different sizes on the wall with athletic tape. The goalkeeper stands 7 to 8 yards back and throws the ball into each box.

APPENDIX: Umpire Signals

1. Time-out

2. Substitution

3. Ten-second count

4. Possession of ball on out-of-bounds — Held whistle / free position

5. Time in

6. Redraw

7. Goal

8. Blocking

9. Offensive foul

10. Held crosse — Empty crosse check

11. Illegal ball off body

12. Illegal check on body

13. Pushing or body contact

14. Rough check

15. No goal

16. Goal circle foul

17. Obstruction of free space to goal

18. Three-second rule

19. Slash

Glossary

Arc: The 8-meter arc is the area in front of each goal circle (or *crease*) inscribed by two lines drawn at 45-degree angles extending from the intersection of the goal circle and the *goal line extended*, connected by an arc marked 8 meters from the goal circle. The 8-meter arc is used to administer major *fouls* such as a 3-second violation.

Attackers: The players who play on the offensive end of the field and primarily *feed* and score.

Backdoor cut: Occurs when an attack player cuts behind her defender toward the goal or ball.

Back side: The side of the field opposite the ball (also known as the *weak side*).

Ball-side: The side of the field that the ball is on. Or defensively, the position between the player being marked and the ball.

Blind pick: A *pick* that isn't set within the visual field of the opponent and that doesn't allow the opponent enough time or space to stop or change direction.

Break out/break: To cut out of the defensive end, with good spacing, when *clearing* the ball.

Catching: To receive or intercept a pass using the stick.

Center circle: A circle with a 3-meter (9 feet, 11 inches) line in the middle, parallel to the *goal lines*, which, if extended, would represent the 50-yard line. This is where the *center draw* occurs.

Center draw: The special situation that starts each game, restarts the game after goals, starts the second half, and any overtime periods.

Change-of-hands dodge: A move executed by the ball carrier, who cradles on her right, pulls her stick across her face, and switches her cradle to her left hand while penetrating the defense. Can be done from right to left or left to right.

Charging: Occurs when the player with the ball pushes into, shoulders, or backs into and makes contact with an opponent who has already established her position.

Checking: Using the stick to make legal contact with an opponent's stick to dislodge the ball.

Clear: A play executed by the defensive team to effectively run or pass the ball from the defensive end of the field to the offensive end of the field. Also, any action taken by a player in the goal circle (or *crease*) to pass or carry the ball out of the goal circle.

Cradling: Using the wrists and arms to keep the ball in the pocket of the stick.

Crease: An 8½-foot circle around each goal that protects the goalie. Offensive and defensive players and their sticks may not enter the crease. Also known as the goal circle.

Critical scoring area: An area at the end of the field (not marked by any lines) where the attacking team is shooting at the goal. Its boundaries are approximately 15 yards around the goal circle and 10 yards behind the goal circle. This area is used to evaluate shooting space and the setup for free positions on certain fouls.

Curling: To shuffle toward the ball in a half-circle pattern to get a better angle for shooting on goal.

Cutting: Movement by the *off-ball* offensive players that helps create space and passing opportunities for the ball carrier. Players try to cut toward the ball carrier, in front of their defenders, in order to receive passes.

Defenders: The players who play on the defensive end of the field.

Defense: The team not in possession of the ball.

Defensive stop: A situation in which the defense has slowed down the offense and prevented a shot on goal.

Dip dodge: A move executed by the ball carrier, who cradles on her right, dips the stick in front of her chest, and switches to her left hand while penetrating the defense. Can be done from right to left or left to right.

Dip save: A save used when the ball is shot between the goalkeeper's shoulder and hip.

Direct free position: Similar to a foul shot in basketball, a direct free position is awarded to an offensive player when a defender commits a major foul (3 seconds, shooting space, etc.) inside the 8-meter arc.

Dodges: Individual moves used to get past a defender.

Double-team: A situation where two players defend one player with the intent of gaining possession of the ball.

Drop step: A small backward step taken to help a defender maintain her positioning or to regain her defensive stance.

Face dodge: A move executed by the ball carrier, who pulls her stick from one side of the head, across the face, and to the other side while penetrating the defense.

Fan: The 12-meter fan is a semicircular area in front of each goal circle bounded by an arc 12 meters from the goal circles. It is used to position players after major and minor fouls.

Fast break: A scoring opportunity created in the *transition* game, which gives the offense a player advantage.

Feeding: Passing the ball to a player who catches and shoots on goal.

Flash: The act of popping toward the goal after setting a *pick*.

Flip save: A save used when the ball is shot between the goalkeeper's hip and knees.

Fouls: Infraction of a rule.

Free space to goal: A path to the goal within the *critical scoring area* as defined by two lines extending from the ball to outside the goal circle.

Goal: The 6-by-6-foot frame with a net into which teams shoot the ball. The goal is defended by the goalie.

Goal cage: See *goal*.

Goal circle: See *crease*.

Goalie: The player inside the *crease* who has the responsibility of defending the goal by preventing shots from crossing the *goal line*. She is also responsible for communicating with the *defense* and starting the *transition* game.

Goal line: A line painted on the field extending from goal post to goal post and of the same width as the goal posts. The line is used to determine if a goal has been scored. The ball must cross the goal line entirely for a goal to be counted.

Goal line extended: An imaginary extension of the *goal line* used as a reference for defenders and attackers when executing moves on the field.

Goal-side: Occurs when a defender is between her opponent and the goal.

Ground ball: A loose ball. Getting possession of ground balls is critical to a team's success.

Head: The plastic portion of the stick extending from the shaft.

Help side: Players on the *off-ball* side who are in a position to support the defenders on the ball side by sliding when necessary.

Hole: The area in the defensive end of the field, in front of the goal.

Indirect free position: When a minor foul is called, a player is awarded an indirect free position, meaning she cannot shoot right away. She must pass the ball to a teammate, or her stick must be checked by a defender's stick before a shot can be taken.

Mark: To defend an opponent, usually within a stick's length.

Midfielders: Players who play in both the offensive and defensive ends of the field. They have offensive and defensive roles and are key components in the *transition* game.

Off-ball movement: Movement by players without the ball to occupy defenders.

Off-ball players: Players without the ball.

Offense: The team in possession of the ball.

Offside: A violation that occurs if a team has more than seven players over the *restraining line* in the offensive end of the field, or more than eight players over the restraining line in the defensive end.

Open player: A player who is not marked by a defender.

Pass and pick away: To pass the ball to a teammate and set a pick for another teammate opposite the ball.

Passing: The technique of throwing the ball to a teammate using the stick in a variety of positions.

Passing lane: Open spaces a cutter can move into to receive a pass.

Penalty lane: The path to the goal that is cleared when a *direct free position* is awarded inside the *critical scoring area* in front of the *goal line*.

Penetration: A *dodge* or movement toward the goal.

Pick: An offensive technique in which one player without the ball comes to a legal position, forcing the defender to take another route. It must be set in the visual field of the opponent and allow the player enough time and space to stop or change direction.

Player-to-player defense: A team defensive strategy in which every defender is responsible for an opposing offensive player.

Pocket: The portion of the stick head created by the mesh or leather stringing. It's where the ball settles in when cradling.

Point behind: The area directly behind the goal. Also known as X.

Pull dodge: See *face dodge*.

Quick stick: A shot on goal in which the player receives the ball and shoots all in one motion, with no cradling.

Restraining line: A solid line at each end of the field 30 yards upfield from the *goal line* that extends fully from one side of the field to the other side.

Riding: A situation in which the offense tries to prevent the defense from *clearing* the ball easily. It is similar to a full-court press in basketball.

Roll dodge: A move executed by the ball carrier, who penetrates the defense by spinning past a defender and attacking the goal.

Roll the crease: An offensive move around the *crease* in which an attacker tries to beat a defender and get a close shot on goal.

Settled offensive set: A situation in which the attack unit maintains possession, passes the ball around the 8-meter *arc*, and *cuts*, sets *picks*, and creates space in an attempt to create quality scoring opportunities.

Shooting space violation: A violation, or foul, in which a player blocks or obstructs the *free space to goal*, between the ball and the goal circle, which denies the attacker the opportunity to shoot safely.

Slashing: Recklessly swinging a stick at an opponent's stick or body with deliberate intent, whether or not the opponent's stick or body is struck.

Slide: A move in which a defender moves off her player to mark a more dangerous player.

Sphere: An imaginary 7-inch area surrounding players' heads. Sticks are not allowed to penetrate this area.

Stick checking: The striking on the corner of an opponent's stick by a defender who is trying to dislodge the ball from the stick. Stick checks should be controlled, short, quick taps.

Strong side: The side of the field that the ball is on.

Sword dodge: A move executed by the ball carrier, who cradles on her right, slides the stick down by her waist, switches to her left hand, and slides her stick back up to cradle on her left. Can also be done left to right.

Three-second violation: A violation in which a defender remains in the 8-meter *arc* for three seconds without marking an opponent or without being within a stick's length of an opponent inside the 8-meter arc.

Trail check: A check from behind.

Transition: The switch from *defense* to *offense* and the movement of the ball from the defensive end to the offensive end.

V-cut: A movement in which the attacker moves into a defender or a defender's space and then explodes away into open space while moving toward the ball. The path of this motion looks like a V.

Warding off: Taking one hand off the stick and using the arm to push off from a defender.

Weak side: The side of the field opposite the ball (also known as the *back side*).

Within a stick's length: Inside a stick's length and an arm's length extended. It's the distance a player must keep between herself and her opponent to be actively marking her.

X: See *point behind*.

Zone defense: A defensive strategy in which the defensive unit is responsible for areas in front of the goal on defense, instead of individual players.

Resources

Associations and Organizations

American Sport Education Program (ASEP)
1607 N. Market St.
Champaign IL 61820
800-747-5698
Fax: 217-351-2674
E-mail: asep@hkusa.com
www.asep.com
ASEP offers educational courses and resources for coaches, directors, and parents to make sports safer, more enjoyable, and valuable for children and young adults. It also publishes books on coaching youth sports.

The Black Women in Sport Foundation
P.O. Box 2610
Philadelphia PA 19130
888-465-1773
Fax: 215-763-2855
E-mail:
info@blackwomeninsport.org
www.blackwomeninsport.org
Founded in 1992 by Tina Sloan Green, the first African-American head coach in the history of women's intercollegiate lacrosse. BWSF is dedicated to facilitating the involvement of black women in every aspect of sport in the United States and around the world, through the "hands-on" development and management of grassroots programs. In the past nine years, BWSF has succeeded in developing mentoring clinics in lacrosse, as well as golf, tennis, soccer, and

fencing for young black women. In addition, BWSF has produced two videos, *Amazing Grace* and *After the Whistle Blows*, along with accompanying teacher and student manuals.

National Alliance for Youth Sports (NAYS)
2050 Vista Pkwy.
West Palm Beach FL 33411
800-729-2057; 800-688-KIDS
    (800-688-5437); 561-684-1141
Fax: 561-684-2546
E-mail: nays@nays.org
www.nays.org
NAYS sponsors nine national programs that educate volunteer coaches, parents, youth sports program administrators, and officials about their roles and responsibilities. Their Web site provides information on education programs including PAYS (Parents Association for Youth Sports), NYSCA (National Youth Sports Officials Association), START SMART, and the Academy for Youth Sports Administrators.

National Federation of State High School Associations (NFHS)
P.O. Box 690
Indianapolis IN 46206
800-776-3462 (to order rule books);
    317-972-6900
Fax: 317-882-5700
www.nfhs.org
Publishes rule books for high school sports, case books (which supplement rule books), and officials' manuals.

**National Youth Sports Safety
Foundation (NYSSF)**
333 Longwood Ave., Suite 202
Boston MA 02115
617-277-1171
Fax: 617-277-2278
E-mail: NYSSF@aol.com
www.nyssf.org
NYSSF is a nonprofit educational
organization whose goal is to reduce
the risks of sports injury to young
people.

Positive Coaching Alliance (PCA)
c/o Stanford Athletic Dept.
Stanford CA 94305-6150
650-725-0024
Fax: 650-725-7242
E-mail: pca@positivecoach.org
www.positivecoach.org
PCA is transforming youth sports so
sports can transform youth.

US Lacrosse
113 W. University Pkwy.
Baltimore MD 21210
410-235-6882
Fax: 410-366-6735
E-mail: info@lacrosse.org
www.lacrosse.org
US Lacrosse is the national governing body of men's and women's
lacrosse. It combines the contribu-
tions and talents of individuals for-
merly involved with a number of in-
dependent national constituencies,
such as the Lacrosse Foundation,
the United States Women's
Lacrosse Association, the National
Junior Lacrosse Association, the
United States Lacrosse Officials Association, United States Lacrosse
Coaches Association, United States
Club Lacrosse Association, the Cen-
tral Atlantic Lacrosse League, and
the National Intercollegiate
Lacrosse Officials Association.

Youth Lacrosse USA (YLUSA)
P.O. Box 10588
Greensboro NC 27404-0588
336-215-4955
Fax: 336-854-1065
E-mail: info@youthlacrosseusa.com
www.youthlacrosseusa.com
YLUSA's goals include energizing
youth to get involved with and learn
to play lacrosse, providing free mini
Web sites for YLUSA-registered
teams, facilitating communication
among coaches and program directors for scheduling, assisting interested parents in developing youth
lacrosse programs, providing
lacrosse tournament, camp, and all-
star team opportunities for youth
players, and developing an on-line
community for youth lacrosse players and program leaders.

Web Sites

Coaching Youth Sports
www.tandl.vt.edu/rstratto/CYS
Virginia Tech's Health and Physical
Education program sponsors this
Web site, which provides coaches,
athletes, and parents with general,
rather than sport-specific, information about skills for youth. The site
also allows browsers to submit
questions.

**National Youth Sports Coaches
Association (NYSCA)**
800-729-2057; 800-688-KIDS
   (800-688-5437); 561-684-1141

www.nays.org/coaches/index.cfm
NYSCA trains volunteer coaches in
all aspects of working with children
and athletics. In addition to training, coaches receive continuing education and insurance coverage and
subscribe to a coaching code of
ethics.

National Youth Sports Officials Association (NYSOA)

800-729-2057; 800-688-KIDS
  (800-688-5437); 561-684-1141
www.nays.org/officials/nysoa.cfm
NYSOA trains volunteer youth
sports officials, providing them with
information on the skills required,
fundamentals of coaching, and
common problems they may
encounter.

Officiating.com

E-mail: Feedback@Officiating.com
www.officiating.com
This Web site offers news, including
updates on rule changes, coaching
philosophy and mechanics, and discussion boards.

US Lacrosse Youth Council

www.lacrosse.org/yth_council.html
The US Lacrosse Youth Council
is charged with promoting girls'
and boys' lacrosse in a safe and
sportsmanlike environment. The
Youth Council has established
a Code of Conduct that emphasizes sportsmanship to players,
coaches, parents, spectators, and
officials. Attendees and participants
in US Lacrosse Youth Council
events are required to sign a contract and pledge to "Honor the
Game."

Lacrosse Stores and Publications

Bacharach

802 Gleneagles Ct.
Towson MD 21286
800-726-2468
Fax: 410-321-0720
E-mail: bachrasin@aol.com
www.bacharach.com
Lacrosse store and catalog com-
pany.

E-Lacrosse

www.e-lacrosse.com
The on-line lacrosse supersite and
store. They have an on-line store
with books.

Great Atlantic Lacrosse Company

Old Wyler's Dock
Box 16872
Chapel Hill NC 27516
800-955-3876
Fax: 800-204-1198
www.lacrosse.com
They produce a catalog and sponsor
many lacrosse events.

Inside Lacrosse

P.O. Box 5570
Towson MD 21285
410-583-8180
Fax: 410-296-8296
www.insidelacrosse.com
A lacrosse magazine and on-line
site.

Lacrosse Magazine

US Lacrosse
113 W. University Pkwy.
Baltimore MD 21210
410-235-6882
Fax: 410-366-6735

E-mail: info@lacrosse.org
www.lacrosse.org/magazine.html
Published eight times a year. US
Lacrosse members receive a sub-
scription to *Lacrosse Magazine*.

Lacrosse Unlimited

2292 Hempstead Turnpike
East Meadow NY 11554
877-932-5229; 800-366-5299
www.lacrosseunltd.com
Lacrosse store, on-line and catalog.

Lax World Lacrosse Superstore

800-PLAY-LAX (800-752-9529)
Fax: 410-561-7278
E-mail: ptmailorder@laxworld.com
www.playlax.com
Lacrosse store, retail and on-line.

Sports Her Way

876 Kenilworth Dr.
Towson MD 21204
888-8HER-WAY (888-843-7929);
410-321-6280
Fax: 410-321-3111
www.sportsherway.com
A store committed to the female
athlete.

360Lacrosse.com

www.360lacrosse.com
On-line store and news center.

Index

Numbers in **bold** refer to pages with illustrations. The glossary and resources have not been indexed.

A

Added Pressure drill, 165
age divisions, 4, 21. *See also* levels of play
aggressive play, 8, 9, 11, 12
Assistant Coach of the Day, 84
assistant coaches, 36–37. *See also* coaches
attackers, **27**, 28
attendance, 19–20
attention, keeping, 17
awards, 99

B

backdoor cuts, 71, 141
back-side position, 80
ball, 24
ball carrier, 68, 70, 72
ball-side position, 81
ball stopper, on stick head, **24–25**
behind-the-back pass, 49
  drill, 116
behind-the-back shot, **59**
blind pick (foul), 31–32, 71
Blob Passing drill, **119**
blocking (foul), 31
blocking passes or shots, **64**
Bounce off the Shaft drill, **110**
Bounce off the Sidewall drill, **110–11**
bounce shots, 58
  saving, 156–57
boundaries, of field, 13, 21–**23**, 24
Box Dodging drill, 51, **126**
Box Double Team drill, 80, **142**
boys' lacrosse. *See* men's lacrosse, versus women's
Breakout drill, **135**

"Bring it In," 15–16, 16–17, 86, 92, 101, 102
Brown, Erin, on her favorite coaches, 34
buddy system, 86

C

canceling practices and games, 39
carpooling, 36, 39
catching, 50–**51**
catching and passing, 46–47
  drills, 114–15, **116–22**
center circle, **23**, 24
center draw, 23, **29–30**, 65–66
Center Draw drill, 65, **138**
centerline, **23**, 24
change-of-hands dodge, 54. *See also* dodging
checking. *See* stick checking
Check Me If You Can drill, 62, 148
chest protector, **150**
clearing ball, 61, **74–75**, 158–60, **159**
  drills, **137**, **147**, 167
Clearing and Throwing drill, 167
coaches. *See also* games; officials; parents; players; practices, about
  equipment checklist, 36
  establishing authority, 15–17, 19, 20
  establishing trust with players, 19
  favorite, 20, 34, 40, 75, 82, 97
  promoting good habits, 15–20
  responsibilities, during games, 100–104
  responsibilities, postpractice, 93
  selecting assistant, 36–37
coaching style, developing, 4–5, 14–15, 69, 75, 90

communication
  from goalie, 146, 147, 149, 160–61
  with officials, 2, 34, 101, 104–5
  with parents, 37, 40, 105
  among players, 80, 81, 141, 143, 146
  with players, 17, 85–86, 90, 91–93, **92**, 102, 103–4
Competitive Ground Balls drill, 43, **123**
complete players, developing, 68, 69
contact, physical, 11, 12
Continuous One-on-One to Goal drill, 130–**31**
Cooke, Kara Ariza, on her favorite coach, 97
cradle, progressive versus traditional, 8, 10–**11**
Cradle and Extended Twirl drill, 41, 113
Cradle and Twirl drill, 41, 113
cradling, 41–43, **42**
  drills, **109–15**
crease, **23**, 24
  fouls around, 33
  movement in, for goalies, **152–53**
  movement outside, for goalies, 162, 165
creativity, and shooting, 9, 59
critical scoring area, 23, 28, 32
criticism
  of officials, 105
  by parents, 105
  of players by coach, 92
  of players by other players and parents, 20, 162
Cross, Dee Fichter, on her favorite coach, 20
Cross the Line drill, **146**
curling (move), 62
  drills, **132**, **147**

Acknowledgments

Loving thanks to John, Ryan, and Devin Tucker, and to Brian, Caroline, and Brian (the younger) Wensel for their unwavering support throughout the writing of this book.

A big, warm collective thank-you goes to:

Trish Dabrowski, for her contribution of the goalkeeping chapter as well as her time and energy editing this book and helping with the photo shoot; Pat Dillon, for her unerring judgment and patience; STX, Inc., in particular Helen Marie Hahn, for a generous contribution of equipment and apparel for the photo shoot; Erin Brown of US Lacrosse, for her direction and expertise; Bill Welch, for a great photo; Tina Sloan Green, for thoughtful reflections; Cherie Greer, for candid comments; Fran Trumbo and Melanie Erhardt, for good-natured guidance during the photo shoot; Ruthie Lavelle, for suggestions and comments; and Stacey Morlang, for help during the photo shoot.

And big hugs to our talented, fabulous, wonderful, terrific, photogenic lacrosse players who appear in the pages of this book: Catherine Barthelme, Maria Brooks, Rachel Goglia, Halle-Paige Gray, Kendall Gray, Kiley Gray, Isabel Harvey, Nolie Krock, Jamie Kunkel, Andrea Pace, Austin Riley, Emily Schroeder, Erin Velez, and Caroline Wensel.

Janine Tucker and Maryalice Yakutchik

About the Authors

Janine Tucker is the head women's lacrosse coach at Johns Hopkins University, a position she's held for ten years. Under her leadership, the team was elevated in 1998 from Division III to Division I and became a nationally ranked top 20 team. In her first year at Johns Hopkins, the team record was 16–1, the best record in the school's history. Her overall record is 111–40. At the Division III Level, she was an Intercollegiate Women's Lacrosse Coaches Association (IWLCA) South Region Coach of the Year for four years. She has coached thirteen All-Americans, along with four Division III Centennial Conference Players of the Year. In addition, Janine has developed and directed girls' lacrosse camps for over a decade, instructing players at every level from 6-year-old beginners to collegiate All-Americans. She also enjoys speaking at clinics nationwide for youth, high school, and collegiate coaches. Prior to Johns Hopkins, she was the assistant women's lacrosse coach at Loyola College, where she was an All-American lacrosse player in 1989. She is a member of the Loyola College Athletic Hall of Fame and was recently inducted into the US Lacrosse Hall of Fame, Greater Baltimore chapter. She graduated in 1989 from Loyola College with a bachelor's degree in communications.

Maryalice Yakutchik is a freelance journalist who writes regularly for the Discovery Channel. Her live expeditions about wildlife and culture appear regularly on Discovery.com and AnimalPlanet.com. She also writes for traditional print media, including newspapers and magazines such as the *Philadelphia Inquirer, Los Angeles Times, Boston Globe, USA Today, Islands,* and *Defenders of Wildlife.* She currently teaches journalism courses at Loyola College. As a student at Temple University (Division I, NCAA) Maryalice was awarded a four-year athletic scholarship for varsity lacrosse and earned a bachelor's degree in journalism and a master's degree in creative writing. She has coached women's lacrosse on the college level, but for the past six years she has devoted her spring seasons to coaching recreation league lacrosse for 6- to 12-year-old girls in her hometown of Monkton, Maryland.